SCOTT PERKINS

EMPATH HEALING

A Guide to Navigating Empathic Sensitivity and Cultivating Emotional Wellness (2024)

Copyright © 2024 by Scott Perkins

All rights reserved. No part of this publication may be reproduced, stored or transmitted in any form or by any means, electronic, mechanical, photocopying, recording, scanning, or otherwise without written permission from the publisher. It is illegal to copy this book, post it to a website, or distribute it by any other means without permission.

First edition

This book was professionally typeset on Reedsy.
Find out more at reedsy.com

Contents

Introduction		v
1	What is an Empath	1
2	Scientific Understanding of Empathy	4
3	History of Empathy	9
4	Importance of Empathy	13
5	Benefits of Being an Empath	19
6	How to Discover and Embrace Your Empath Gift?	24
7	Are you an Empath?	27
8	Understanding and Embracing Your Gift	31
9	Normalizing and Maintaining Your Gift	35
10	Trust Your Intuition	39
11	Types of Empaths	45
12	Empath and Relationsh	50
13	Tips for Empaths in Intimate Relationship	54
14	Tools for Transformation and Spiritual Growth	58
15	Your Guide to Healing Meditation	62
16	Empath Healing	69
17	How Empathy Works	74
18	Different Empathy Levels	80
19	Which Areas of the Empathic Lives?	86
20	Are Empaths Born or Developed?	90
21	Emotional Intelligence and Empathy	94
22	Different Ways to Overcome Anxiety as An Empath	98
23	Change Your Mindset	103
24	How to Get Rid of Toxic and Negative People and Negative...	107
25	Finding Empathic Joy	113

26 The Overall Experience of a Person's Empathic Healing   117
Conclusion   121

Introduction

If you are perusing this book, I presume that you are aware of being an Empath, are in the process of understanding it, or know someone who falls into this category. Regardless, you've come to the right place to enhance your knowledge, as this book provides the most current information on the subject.

The primary point to grasp for anyone intrigued by this topic is that being an empath is an inherent part of one's genetic composition. It is a lifelong trait, likely passed down from one or both parents, and it should not be perceived as an illness, disease, or psychological disorder that can be treated with medication or therapy.

But there's no need to be distressed; you're not alone. Statistics indicate that approximately 1 in 20 individuals are empaths or highly sensitive individuals. If you're seeking a solution to this 'condition,' you may be disappointed because, as mentioned earlier, this trait is not something that can be cured. However, the purpose of this book is to educate empaths on how to effectively manage this trait, enabling them to harness its benefits and create a more joyful future.

In addition to empaths, there is another group commonly referred to as Highly Sensitive People (HSP). For the purpose of this book, these terms will be used interchangeably, although some believe there is a distinction between the two. The information in this book is applicable to both empaths and HSPs, as both types share a heightened sense of feeling. The book delves into the topics of feeling and sensitivity, so don't be discouraged if you identify with a different term; this book offers information on a variety of related subjects.

The central goal of this book is to help individuals recognize that being an empath is a gift to the world, not a hindrance. Unfortunately, many of us have never been taught how to harness and work with this attribute. Like anything in life, lack of understanding can lead to confusion or fear. Having personally experienced the challenges of growing up with this tendency and feeling different from others, I encountered numerous personal lows. It wasn't until I recognized the need to understand myself better and embrace all aspects of me that I could unlock the true strength that comes with being an empath. Now, I view it as a rare gift, something not everyone possesses. Learning to use this attribute has improved my relationships, allowing me to better understand others without being overwhelmed by their emotions, a struggle I faced for most of my life.

This book begins by examining empaths and the challenges they face in greater detail. With these insights, we can uncover emotional pain accumulated over years of living with this trait. Addressing this emotional wounding is crucial for moving forward and positively impacting the future. The book explores various methods of healing and overcoming past traumas, offering a survival guide with tools that empaths can use to function at their best while keeping anxiety, negativity, and fear at bay. Practical exercises in the book are presented in easily understandable sections that can be implemented almost immediately.

Empaths and sensitives also contend with overwhelming environments, such as crowded places and the collective energy of the planet. In a journey to conquer and harness their natural empathic abilities, individuals become acclimated and prepared to address the challenges faced by people in the world. An empath's life mission is of the highest purpose, and it's crucial to remember this, as it is this very reason that will provide the strength to endure.

1

What is an Empath

The term 'empath' has gained increased recognition in recent years for various reasons. Many individuals may have encountered this term through popular culture outlets such as television, movies, and literature. Numerous fictional characters have been labeled as 'empaths,' though the accuracy of their portrayal remains a subject of debate. Another contributing factor to the widespread awareness of this term is the growing popularity of personality tests. While some of these tests concentrate on psychology-defined personality traits, others explore different aspects such as psychic abilities and spiritual inclinations. Within the realm of these personality tests, the label 'empath' is utilized to describe a specific kind of person—one who possesses a heightened sensitivity to their intuition.

Undoubtedly, the definition of an empath varies significantly across different sources, leading the average person to inquire, "What is an empath?" This section will address prevalent misconceptions surrounding empaths while elucidating the fundamental characteristics that truly define what an empath is.

Common Misunderstandings About Empaths

The portrayal of empathy in popular culture encompasses a wide array of characteristics, skills, and traits. While some of these depictions are positive, others are exaggerated, if not entirely false and unrealistic. This is largely because movies, TV shows, and books prioritize creating entertaining and captivating characters over exploring the authentic nature of empathy in real life. It is crucial to distinguish between the empathy depicted in pop culture and its genuine manifestation.

One prevalent misconception is the belief that empaths can read minds as effortlessly as reading a book. This idea gained popularity through the character Deanna Troi in Star Trek: The Next Generation, who belonged to a race of empaths called Betazoids. Despite the show suggesting Betazoids could read minds and communicate telepathically, Deanna's abilities were only half as potent due to her mixed heritage. In reality, empaths cannot read minds but may sense strong emotions.

Another misconception is that empaths fully comprehend and control their abilities. Contrary to this belief, empaths don't always understand the source of their feelings, especially in the midst of conversations or events. They cannot interpret emotional signals with absolute certainty, debunking the notion that empaths possess an innate understanding of every emotional nuance they experience.

Some portrayals in pop culture take empathic intuition to extreme levels, suggesting empaths can foresee future events. Star Wars, for instance, depicts Jedi Masters using the force for intuitive assessments. However, the reality is that empaths rely on whether a choice or situation feels good or bad and do not possess the ability to predict distant or future events.

The fanciful idea that all empaths have mystical personalities, speaking in riddles and hearing the voice of the universe, is another misconception. While some empaths may appear more mystical due to their heightened emotional awareness, others may seem less so, appearing normal or even detached. The notion that empaths have a secret language and can recognize each other by their aura is pure fiction.

The Genuine Nature of Empaths

Despite the exaggerated and fantastical depictions in pop culture, empaths are individuals worthy of admiration. A confident and well-functioning empath stands out not only in terms of personality but also in terms of their unique abilities. While empaths communicate using spoken words and do not hear the voice of the universe, they possess valuable skills that can seem extraordinary.

One common empathic ability is the knack for forming accurate first impressions of people, seeing beyond surface appearances. This skill, though less flashy than telepathy, can prevent falling victim to deceptive individuals. Empaths rely on intuition to assess a person's character, discerning what lies beneath spoken words.

Trust issues are another genuine aspect of empaths, arising from the conflict between intuition and rational thinking. Empaths may receive conflicting first impressions of a person, one based on appearances and another based on intuition. Trusting the intuitive impression becomes a challenge, especially when it contradicts the outwardly safe and good appearance of an individual.

Empaths also possess the ability to sense the energy of a situation, which, upon closer examination, makes logical sense. Using intuition, empaths can perceive the emotions of individuals as well as the overall energy of a situation. This enables them to sense negativity or danger in a particular scenario.

In essence, an empath is someone with heightened intuition, enabling them to perceive things beyond the scope of physical senses. While this may seem mystical, it is a commonplace ability. Despite its positive applications, being an empath comes with challenges, making their lives uniquely complex and extraordinary.

2

Scientific Understanding of Empathy

Empathy involves a heightened sensitivity to subtle energy, a concept that extends beyond Albert Einstein's formula. This energy encompasses everything, as affirmed by conventional science, which establishes that even emotions are manifestations of energy. Empaths must acquire the skill of navigating this energy field.

This universal energy has been acknowledged and examined since ancient times, known by diverse names reflecting regional and cultural distinctions. In China, it is called chi; in Japan, ki; and in Greece, pneuma. Despite these variations, these terms all point to the same pervasive force responsible for the creation of all things. It's crucial to recognize that this energy is eternal, undergoing transmutation rather than ceasing to exist.

Ubiquitous in nature, this energy exists within and around every individual. Some even assert that this omnipresent force is synonymous with God. Importantly, as energy fluctuates, so do emotions. This fluctuation is evident in personal experiences, where emotions shift from sadness to happiness, and in interactions with others, where varying energy qualities can be expected. Empaths must cultivate flexibility to adeptly navigate these diverse energy states.

SCIENTIFIC UNDERSTANDING OF EMPATHY

Given that emotions are essentially energy, empaths should possess a profound understanding of this fundamental force. The most effective way to deepen this understanding is through direct sensory experiences. Consequently, it becomes imperative for empaths to learn how to feel and perceive this energy firsthand.

How to Experience Energy Sensation

This specific activity provides a means to perceive energy through your hands. The procedure is outlined as follows:

1. Begin by relaxing.
2. Position your hands in front of you as if holding an imaginary ball.
3. Inhale deeply and gradually move your hands apart.
4. Exhale slowly, bringing your hands as close together as possible without touching. Repeat steps 3-4 as necessary.

By engaging in this exercise, you can develop the ability to sense energy with your hands. If you are a beginner, it may take several minutes or repetitions before you notice any sensations. Energy manifestations often include heat, pressure, or a tingling feeling on your hands. Recognizing any of these sensations indicates that you are likely sensing energy.

It's important to understand that everything possesses an energy field, commonly referred to as an aura. This energetic field surrounds all entities, including humans, animals, plants, and even inanimate objects. To further explore and test this exercise, try feeling the aura. After sensitizing your hands through the exercise, attempt to sense your own aura by placing your hand above your forearms and gradually moving closer. You should feel some pressure or warmth, signifying your aura. Additionally, you can extend this practice to feeling the aura of another person by standing a few feet away, facing outward with your hands, and moving towards the subject. Soon, you'll sense the subject's aura on your palms.

Auras consist of multiple layers, with four main layers identified in the human aura: the etheric aura (closest to the body), mental aura, emotional aura, and spiritual aura. In practices like psychism, individuals sense a person's aura to aid in treating illnesses, as it is believed that diseases first manifest in the aura before affecting the physical body. Furthermore, a person's aura reflects their mental and emotional states, making the ability to read and sense auras a valuable skill for empaths.

How to Perceive the Aura

Learning to see the aura can be a fascinating skill that enhances your understanding of individuals. There are two primary methods to perceive the aura: physically and psychically.

Physically seeing the aura should not be considered unusual; it's believed that everyone saw their aura in their youth. With enough practice, you can relearn this skill. Follow these steps:

1. Choose a neutral background, preferably white, in a dimly lit or pitch-black environment.
2. Relax and extend your hand in front of you against the background.
3. Focus on one of your fingers using soft focus (peripheral vision), allowing you to see a faint light emitting from your hand. Initially, you might observe a white field of energy, but with practice, you can discern other colors like blue, red, and yellow.
4. Extend this technique to observe the auras of other people using your peripheral vision.

Note that aura colors are subjective, and individuals may perceive them differently. Experiment with this technique, associating certain colors with specific emotions or energy qualities. Understanding aura colors can help you discern the energy and emotional state of individuals, enabling you to make informed decisions about your interactions with them.

Perceiving the Aura Psychically

To perceive the aura psychically, you need a well-developed intuition. Follow these steps:

1. Look at a person and memorize their facial features, clothing, etc.
2. Close your eyes, visualize the person, and affirm your intention to see their aura.
3. In your mind's eye, the person's aura should gradually appear. Take note and interpret what you see.

This technique requires practice, and it's crucial to pay attention not only to aura colors but also to their shapes. If you don't sense or see the aura initially, don't be discouraged; consistent practice is key, especially for empaths.

How to Safeguard Against Energy Drainers

Empaths face a higher susceptibility to energy drainers. So, what exactly are these energy drainers? They are individuals who extract energy from you like a parasite. You may have experienced feeling depleted after engaging with such individuals – a clear manifestation of energy vampirism. Typically, this occurs when interacting with someone harboring negative energy. The underlying reason is that those with a lower vibrational frequency absorb energy from those vibrating at a higher frequency. Negative energy characterizes low vibration, while positive energy characterizes high vibration. Consequently, when engaging with a negative person, it is often you who feels drained. Fortunately, there are preventive measures you can adopt to shield yourself from these so-called energy drainers. The initial step involves avoiding negative individuals, or at least maintaining distance while you are still mastering control over your empathic abilities. In unavoidable encounters with negative individuals, employ a defensive technique by mentally constructing a barrier between you and the negativity. Follow these steps:

1. Visualize a robust wall during interaction with the negative person, firmly believing that no negative energy can penetrate this powerful barrier. Maintain confidence in its efficacy; don't harbor doubts.

2. Seize control of the conversation to prevent the negative person from transferring their negativity. Assume a leading role in steering the conversation.

3. Create a protective bubble shield as an additional preventive measure.

Develop a familiarity with perceiving and sensing energy, as empaths primarily engage with energy, even if it manifests as emotions. Understanding energy better enhances your comprehension of the people you interact with. Empathy revolves around emotions, and emotions are essentially energy. A common error is being overly sensitive to others while neglecting one's own sensitivity. If you notice that external energies are affecting you and making it challenging to manage emotions, step back and take a break. Some empaths realize this too late, after the energy has already taken its toll. Thus, heightened sensitivity to energy is crucial. Don't just sense it; pay close attention to the emotions transmitted by others. Positive emotions pose no issue, but when dealing with negativity, it is essential to shield yourself.

In encounters with negative individuals or psychic vampires, remind yourself not to form excessive attachments.

3

History of Empathy

Investigating Empathy and its Neurobiological Foundation

When exploring the characteristics of compassion and empathy, and the brain regions influencing these responses, a central question arises: is empathy a product of inherent neural wiring or learned discipline? Can compassion and empathy be cultivated, or are individuals inherently bound by a predetermined threshold, regardless of life experiences? If these qualities can be nurtured over time, are there daily practices, exercises, or routines that may mitigate or alter tendencies towards selfishness, narcissism, sociopathy, or psychopathy? Conversely, are there habits that reinforce or exacerbate these conditions? If we can impart compassion and empathy to our children, it becomes a responsibility for shaping future generations.

In October 2013, the Max Planck Institute for Human and Cognitive Brain Sciences conducted a study on the neurobiological underpinnings of specific behaviors. The research delves into how neurobiological roots, shaped by past experiences, impact an individual's capacity for empathy and compassion. Concurrently, a September 2013 study from the University of Chicago explored the neurobiological origins of psychopathic behaviors. Insights from these studies provide crucial clues on how to enhance empathetic and compassionate responses at a neural level. Remarkably, both studies suggest that empathy and compassion can indeed be learned.

The initial study in October 2013, reported in the Journal of Neuroscience, proposed that a predisposition toward egocentric behavior is intrinsic to human nature. However, the researchers also concluded that the brain contains a mechanism, specifically the right supramarginal gyrus, which identifies a lack of empathy and prompts corrective actions in situations influenced by egocentric tendencies.

The right supramarginal gyrus, situated at the junction of the parietal, temporal, and frontal lobes, plays a pivotal role in analyzing emotions. It distinguishes between one's emotional state and the emotions of others, serving as the seat of both empathy and compassion. Surprisingly, the study found that individuals with disrupted supramarginal gyrus function exhibited reduced empathy, particularly in quick decision-making scenarios.

The team, led by Tania Singer, emphasized that humans tend to use their own emotional state as a reference when assessing others, leading to an inherent egocentricity that distorts the understanding of differing emotions. The right supramarginal gyrus, by revealing disparities between self-perceptions and perceptions of others, contributes to humility.

Interestingly, the Max Planck study revealed that individuals leading a luxurious lifestyle often display a lower threshold and diminished capacity for empathy. A comfortable existence appears to hinder the proper functioning of the supramarginal gyrus on a neurobiological level. This suggests that experiencing ease in life makes it challenging to empathize with the struggles and hardships of others.

To test this, Singer's team conducted experiments pairing participants subjected to either pleasant or unpleasant stimuli. The findings indicated that those accustomed to agreeable stimuli had a lower neurobiological response to the suffering of others. The tactile and visual stimuli experiments demonstrated that individuals in a luxurious environment found it more difficult to empathize when life was exceedingly easy.

In summary, these studies shed light on the neurobiological roots of empathy and compassion, highlighting the role of the right supramarginal gyrus. Understanding these mechanisms could pave the way for interventions and educational approaches to foster empathy and compassion, ultimately benefiting society as a whole.

In the conducted experiment, each participant was tasked with providing a brief evaluation of their own emotions in comparison to the person seated next to them. When participants were exposed to similar stimuli, they found it easy to gauge the emotional state of the other person. In cases where both participants encountered different types of negative stimuli, participant A could accurately assess the impact of the negative stimuli on participant B, and vice versa.

The most significant change in empathetic response occurred when participants were subjected to varying stimuli. When one participant experienced positive circumstances while the other faced negative ones, empathy levels plummeted for the participant with positive stimuli. The positive emotions of one participant distorted their perception of the other participant's experience, leading to an underestimation of the severity of their circumstances.

This suggests that when participant A experienced positive stimuli while participant B faced negative stimuli, participant A tended to underestimate the seriousness of B's situation, resulting in more positive assessments than B's actual condition. Conversely, participant B's assessments of A's circumstances and feelings were less positive than A's actual state.

Traditionally, it was assumed that people primarily rely on their own emotions for empathy, but this holds true only when the right supramarginal gyrus doesn't inhibit the naturally predisposed egocentric processes. This study implies that the supramarginal gyrus plays a crucial role in developing empathy and compassion. Individuals with lower supramarginal gyrus activity may struggle to feel empathy for those in dissimilar situations.

Examining the neurological basis of empathy deficiency leads to psychopathy, a personality disorder characterized by a lack of remorse or empathy, along with traits like glibness, callousness, and manipulation. Shallow affect, exhibiting a minimal response to emotional stimuli, is a key feature of psychopathy.

Research on participants with psychopathy revealed a lack of brain activation in regions associated with empathy, concern, and compassionate decision-making when imagining others in pain. A study by the University of Chicago identified neurological roots for psychopathic tendencies, indicating that highly psychopathic individuals can feel pain themselves but struggle to empathize when imagining it happening to others. The diagnostic tool used in these studies, the PCL-R, is commonly employed to assess various degrees of psychopathic behavior.

4

Importance of Empathy

Engaging in the dynamic human culture contributes to the cultivation of diverse emotions, moods, and habits that impact our behavior. Empathy is one such disposition, possibly instinctual, yet modern surroundings with their fast-paced nature offer some protective factors. Individuals possessing empathy are adept at fostering, constructing, and attaining meaningful and wholesome connections. In essence, empathy serves as a significant ally in establishing relationships, be they professional or personal.

Empathy stands out as a crucial attribute for a prosperous life, intertwining with the capacity to harbor well-balanced emotions and effectively navigate daily challenges and conflicts. It involves forging genuine connections with subordinates, peers, and superiors. In the professional realm, empathy enables managers to enhance communication with their teams.

While empathy holds paramount importance for professional advancement and personal growth, caution is warranted against excessive immersion in others' perspectives, leading to challenges in distinguishing between personal and professional boundaries with subordinates and peers. Like any skill, empathy is partly innate and partly acquired through learning, allowing for development over time. Generally, task-oriented and highly assertive executives may exhibit limited empathic capacity, hindering their relationships and compromising overall outcomes.

A Mindset Linked to an Innate Instinct

Given that humans are inherently social beings, accustomed by nature to coexist with their peers, life itself is an integral part of our defining essence. Therefore, living in complete isolation, detached from all civilization, is exceedingly challenging, if not nearly impossible.

Various behaviors manifest within this shared existence, reflecting the diverse aspects of human nature. These can range from profound sensitivity and compassion to outright selfishness and malevolence. Among these behaviors, empathy stands out as a crucial quality. Empathy is the capacity for an individual to feel or resonate with the suffering of others, often seen as an abstract manifestation of solidarity. It allows us to perceive when another person is experiencing distress and, in turn, prompts us to take action, either assisting them in moving forward or offering solace.

To comprehend why an individual possesses empathy, it's essential to recognize its connection to the cultivation of specific forms of emotional intelligence. This emotional intelligence enables us to be responsive and receptive to both our own and others' suffering. While some individuals may grow up without any inclination to nurture emotional or even cognitive intelligence, others exhibit heightened sensitivity to the experiences of others, either due to inherent traits or life experiences. Consequently, these individuals tend to demonstrate greater empathy in situations of pain or hardship.

The Importance of Empathy Towards Our Peers

In contemporary societies, the prevailing individualistic mindset often prioritizes personal well-being over communal welfare. Nevertheless, fostering empathy is imperative for it to become a widespread and intrinsic attitude among us, as it significantly impacts the well-being of a community. This is because acts of support, attentiveness to others, companionship in their struggles, and providing assistance collectively define our humanity and contribute to our enrichment as individuals.

Here are the key aspects of practicing empathy in everyday life:

1. **Unity:**
It's a misconception to associate the term "solidarity" solely with volunteer work. Demonstrating solidarity involves acknowledging and assisting others in times of need. Instead of turning a blind eye to friends, family, or colleagues requiring help, extend your support whenever possible.

2. **Esteem:**
Recognizing that everyone chooses their life path and respecting those decisions is fundamental for human interaction. Despite the prevalent lack of universal acceptance, it's crucial to act with courtesy and kindness towards others. Respect diverse choices in lifestyle, religion, sexual orientation, political beliefs, and other potentially contentious subjects. Embracing differences fosters greater harmony in the world.

3. **Attuning to Essence:**
Empathy emphasizes the significance of truly listening to people. This involves attentively hearing, understanding, accepting, and expressing your opinions respectfully. This approach indicates a genuine concern for allowing everyone's perspectives to be heard, creating an essential foundation for healthy debates.

4. **Continuous Learning:**
Lifelong evolution is indispensable, requiring a commitment to ongoing education. Actively engage in sharing knowledge with fellow professionals, participate in constructive discussions, read extensively, pursue additional

studies, and seek coaching opportunities. Investing in continual education and diverse learning methods ensures regular personal growth.

5. **Community Spirit:**
Collective awareness holds immense importance, both within business environments and society at large. Beyond just teamwork skills, community spirit instills the value of respecting diverse opinions and inclusivity for everyone, especially those with fewer opportunities. This collective approach is crucial for fostering positive coexistence in society.

Are you aware of the significance of being an empathetic individual? If not, you now possess valuable insights to incorporate into your daily life. Ensure that you exhibit positive traits related to the aspects discussed here. These attributes not only contribute to your mental well-being but are also crucial for fostering positive social interactions within and outside the professional realm.

Given that people are inherently social beings, interactions with others are inevitable. In such instances, empathy plays a pivotal role for several reasons:

1. **Empathy Facilitates Communication:**
Empathetic individuals can connect with others, making it easier to comprehend their intentions in communication. Accurately perceiving and understanding others is fundamental for smooth communication, minimizing misunderstandings in both personal and professional contexts.

2. **Empathy Creates Harmonious Relationships:**
Particularly essential in friendships, partnerships, and family bonds, empathy ensures enduring relationships by preventing major conflicts. Understanding others' perspectives is the first step, followed by accepting their attitudes and views, paving the way for conflict resolution and sustained harmony.

3. **Self-Reflection and Empathy:**
Empathy, coupled with self-honesty, provides valuable tools for self-reflection. Beyond external interactions, it aids in understanding one's thoughts and emotions, fostering personal growth. Mindfulness and empathy together enable continuous self-improvement.

4. **Empathy in Leadership:**
Empathy, when combined with technical skills, influence, creativity, and effective communication, becomes an indispensable quality for effective leadership. Leaders who lack empathy may inadvertently exhibit selfish behavior, hindering team cohesion and creativity. Empathetic leaders, on the other hand, consider individual needs and differences, fostering a positive and creative work environment.

By applying empathy, not only do you enhance your interactions with others, but you also gain a deeper understanding of yourself. This emotional knowledge and vocabulary, developed through recognizing personal reactions, enable better recognition of emotions in others and facilitate meaningful conversations.

Encouraging you to integrate empathy into your conversations, you'll likely observe improvements in your relationships. Moreover, demonstrating empathetic qualities complements your personal branding, proving your commitment to career advancement and interpersonal growth.

Quality relationships with others, whether friends, colleagues, or family, benefit from the application of empathy. It provides an opportunity for self-discovery, requiring emotional knowledge and vocabulary, enhancing communication and understanding in various life situations.

In leadership, empathy stands as a cornerstone alongside technical skills, influence, creativity, and communication. Striving to embody empathetic leadership contributes to a positive work culture, individual development, and overall team success. Though not every leader may naturally possess these qualities, aspiring towards them is crucial for effective leadership. Through tools focusing on emotional intelligence, self-confidence, humanized management, and behavioral trend identification, individuals can enhance their personal and professional performance, aspiring to become the empathetic leaders of the future.

5

Benefits of Being an Empath

The concept of this 'gift' is often perceived as a burden, and a significant portion of this book has concentrated on the unfavorable aspects of being an empath. However, this emphasis was crucial to assist you in comprehending and managing yourself better, empowering you to fully embrace and utilize this gift. Many qualities labeled as 'negative' are, in reality, also positive but are viewed from a different perspective. It's akin to a double-edged sword, where our goal is to effectively counteract the adverse effects by transforming them into positive advantages.

Empaths have experienced heightened sensitivity since birth, leading to the formation of neural connections in their brains to compensate for their natural alertness and sensitivity. These neural pathways represent connections formed through repeated actions, and the more an action is repeated, the stronger these connections become, eventually solidifying into habits. For instance, if you habitually avoided eye contact due to the overwhelming emotions you felt, your brain would establish connections to avoid eye contact in future encounters, gradually making it an unconscious habit.

Consequently, many empathic behaviors are deeply ingrained, rooted in years of repeated actions as a means of self-defense. Changing these deeply embedded behaviors and beliefs can prove immensely challenging. The most straightforward approach is to build upon existing tendencies, reinforcing new behaviors by establishing new connections along established neural pathways.

The initial step involves wholeheartedly accepting and embracing this trait as a gift. This acceptance is essential for tapping into its power. For many years, I detested this trait, attempting to overcome it under the misconception that it was psychological programming inherited from my mother. However, I eventually realized it was a genetic predisposition towards sensitivity passed down from my mother. Acceptance became the key to working with and understanding this aspect of myself.

Resisting this trait led to numerous challenges throughout my life, from extreme shyness in my early years to heightened sensitivity and anxiety in adulthood. Only by embracing this part of myself did I begin to function at a higher level. Learning how to protect myself became instrumental in finding greater happiness—an outcome I wish for you as well.

Being an empath often brings a sense of being different, misunderstood, and excluded from normal society. Yet, as I discovered, we are special. Understanding these gifts starts with paying closer attention to oneself through non-judgment and non-resistance. For example, I used to despise my expansive aura as it made me highly noticeable, a challenge for my extreme shyness. However, as I learned to work with this gift, I realized I could influence the energy of a room with my presence. People began expressing gratitude for my kindness and sharing deeply personal thoughts after just a brief encounter.

This gift, however, should be wielded through conscious decision-making. Establishing boundaries allowed me to build self-confidence and trust in myself. Animals seemed to connect with me, and I discovered visual creativity, a love for writing, and a unique ability to communicate with others. My ongoing journey of self-discovery has been incredibly rewarding, and I genuinely believe the same is possible for every empath out there.

Your Skills

Possessing the capacity to establish deeper connections with others, to empathize and truly comprehend their perspectives, is an invaluable trait. This ability extends across various professions, ranging from sales and medicine to therapy. Individuals with this skill are unlikely to face difficulty in securing employment, as the world increasingly values genuinely caring and understanding individuals. Empaths, known for their heightened introspection, can channel this sensitivity inward, fostering intuition that proves highly beneficial when the mind is free from mental distractions. Cultivating trust in this intuition over time serves as a guiding force, facilitating a more directed life path. This innate sixth sense not only aids in connection but also unveils one's genuine life calling and deepest purpose.

Healing

The natural talent for self-healing and aiding others is a unique skill. To truly master this ability, it requires the development of emotional detachment. Stepping into someone else's shoes, sensing and feeling their experiences, is a precious skill that, although challenging, allows for treating others with enhanced compassion. Empaths, naturally inclined toward professions involving healing, find fulfilling careers as therapists and practitioners of alternative methods like Reiki and hypnotherapy.

They can also facilitate healing by attuning to another's emotions, drawing out pain through a joint transmutation of emotional trauma. Skilled empaths can uncover concealed emotional issues by sensing and helping individuals work through their emotional blocks, providing valuable guidance for inner healing, particularly when someone is grappling with a specific issue.

Telepathy/Psychic Abilities

There is a prevailing belief in the existence of psychic abilities within everyone, enabling glimpses into unrelated past or future events. Empaths, attuned to energy subtleties, naturally possess telepathic talents, including precognition for predicting future events. Proficient empaths engage in various levels of psychic work, such as Mediumship for connecting with spirits or using their ability to understand animals at a profound level.

Some empaths specialize in Geomancy, honing their skills to feel the Earth's energies, predict water flow, and forecast weather patterns. While it may be puzzling to comprehend the purpose of these abilities in relation to one's life journey, using natural talents, abilities, and interests as a guide can lead to a profound understanding of personal truths.

Raising the Vibrational Frequency

Simply by existing on Earth, empaths contribute to transmuting negative energies, making them indispensable. In times of heightened negativity, empaths play a crucial role in absorbing and neutralizing such energies. Elevating the planet's vibrational frequency is considered a spiritual undertaking, achievable through self-love and self-care. By nurturing overall health, individuals amplify their natural talents, and by pursuing personal interests, they contribute positive vibrations to the planet.

Choosing actions rooted in love ensures a constant state of happiness. Shifting from survival mode to thriving begins by bravely taking steps toward goals and dreams. Empaths possess great strength, forged through life's challenges, which should be harnessed to propel them forward and positively impact the planet.

Sixth Sense

Empaths perceive the world through emotions, feelings, and energies, essentially possessing a sixth sense. Losing this ability would leave them feeling stuck, as it encompasses various gifts often taken for granted. Being able to discern truth from lies or sensing others' pain for potential healing are forms of guidance within this sixth sense. Although help may be dismissed at times, recognizing that some individuals need to undergo suffering for personal growth and awakening is crucial. Challenges, though formidable, lead to growth and strength, akin to conquering a mountain. The view from the top and the inner wisdom gained make overcoming such difficulties truly worthwhile.

6

How to Discover and Embrace Your Empath Gift?

Having gone through the content, experiencing life as an empath proves to be both physically and emotionally draining, making it seem more like a burden than a gift. Acknowledging this weight is the initial step toward embracing your empathic abilities. To fully embrace your gift, it becomes crucial to acquire self-care skills that prevent exhaustion. This necessitates an investment of time and effort in mastering effective coping mechanisms. Once adept at managing your empathic nature, you can utilize this gift for personal growth and positive influence in your surroundings.

Given the constant barrage of overwhelming emotions and stress, it becomes imperative to actively eliminate the negative energy you may attract. The coping techniques learned should seamlessly integrate into your daily routine, revealing the genuine value of your endowed gift.

While being an empath is not an ailment or a curse, it can be contentious and induce discomfort, leading some to suppress it. Analogous to the Alcoholics or Narcotics Anonymous slogan—acknowledging the problem as the first step towards recovery—you, as an empath, must first admit and take pride in your empathic nature. Although seemingly small, this acknowledgment significantly reduces the stress associated with concealing your gift.

To alleviate the challenges of empathic living, sufficient rest is paramount. Establishing a regular sleep-wake cycle ensures restful nights, while breaks throughout the day, coupled with relaxation and deep breathing exercises, provide immediate relief from accumulated stress.

Avoiding consistently overstimulating environments proves challenging but is essential for an empath. When unavoidable, emotional and mental preparation beforehand helps swiftly alleviate stress induced by the surrounding energies.

Recognizing that social media and the internet are highly stimulating, periodic breaks from their energy are recommended. Absorbing others' energy doesn't necessitate physical presence, emphasizing the need for balancing online interactions.

Additionally, incorporating a stress relief routine is advised, tailored to individual preferences—whether through reading motivational books, receiving massages, visiting a spa, engaging in aromatherapy, or enjoying a warm bath.

Here are some valuable suggestions to help you fully embrace your unique gift.

Appreciate and Respect Your State of Awareness

Empaths often feel pressure due to their distinctiveness. The challenges arise from societal expectations to conform to established norms and values. When others misunderstand you, it's easy to internalize their disapproval as a burden. Being empathic is not only normal but also a valuable connection with yourself on physical and spiritual levels. Embracing this gift is essential for survival, as it heightens your awareness of potential dangers to yourself or your family.

Differentiate Between Thought and Empathic Awareness

Just as you can observe the contrast between day and night visually, it's challenging to pinpoint empathic awareness since it's felt and experienced internally. Recognizing this disparity allows you to view your gift as a blessing rather than a curse. Attaining self-knowledge involves distinguishing when the mind dominates with its thoughts. Understanding that feelings and thoughts are distinct liberates you. This awareness empowers you to defend against energetic influences instead of being drawn into them.

Have Confidence in Your Intuition

Many empaths awakening to their gifts tend to disregard their gut instincts. It's crucial not to ignore them; your intuition is consistently accurate. Acknowledging a feeling doesn't require a complete understanding of the situation. Trusting your intuition allows you to accept the profound internal connection that goes beyond surface-level comprehension.

7

Are you an Empath?

Empaths, put simply, are individuals with heightened sensitivity. However, there is much more to being an empath than this basic definition suggests—aspects that are often overlooked or blurred due to the world's tendency to oversimplify matters into black and white. Being an empath isn't a conscious choice between two extremes; it's not a choice at all. One is either born as an empath or is not.

Empaths consciously or subconsciously feel the emotions of others through their sensitivity. This means the emotions they perceive from others are not always within their control. An empath can discern the emotions of a person without needing to hear them speak. There are instances where empaths can even sense the true emotion behind distorted sounds. Regardless of a person speaking in a cheerful tone, an empath can detect if they are depressed. Empaths, when people hear voices, feel empathic.

Various empaths can read emotions through people's eyes, sense feelings through smell, and some even abstain from eating meat, feeling the suffering of animals. For empaths, feelings manifest through sight, sound, taste, smell, and physical contact. The ability to sense things even without intending to feel them is an inherent enhancement to all their senses.

Empaths' abilities extend beyond emotions; they can sense physical suffering and may adopt such illnesses. Occasionally, the physical pain, aches, and fatigue experienced by empaths result from absorbing too many emotions from others. Despite being frequently misunderstood, empaths are spiritually connected to humanity and often harbor enduring hope for its betterment.

People have approached me, asking about their abilities. I respond with a question, prompting them to contemplate their perceived abilities. Sometimes, the response is uncertainty, leading to an explanation of why the question is posed. If one already senses having an ability, there must be a reason—perhaps glimpses out of the corner of the eye or premonitions of future events. Keeping a journal is recommended to determine one's abilities. Note all encountered phenomena for about a month, then review to identify inherent abilities.

Belief in one's gifts enhances the experiences, but fear necessitates learning to stand up against frightening encounters. Sharing a personal experience, seven years ago, an attempt at sensory deprivation resulted in overwhelming fear and a realization of the need for self-protection. Before attempting to develop abilities, learning to protect oneself is crucial. Developing abilities, especially through methods like sensory deprivation, is better done with company for protection and a sense of security.

To discover one's abilities, one must open their mind, accepting the possibility of possessing unexpected or frightening abilities. Personal experience underscores the importance of embracing all gifts, gaining control over them, and acknowledging that avoiding certain abilities may have unwanted consequences. The story emphasizes the need to be open to all gifts and gain control over them to prevent undesirable impacts on life.

WHY IT'S BENEFICIAL TO CULTIVATE YOUR PSYCHIC CAPABILITY

The awakening of psychic abilities varies from person to person, driven by diverse factors that lack a universal explanation. Each individual's catalyst for unlocking these abilities differs; however, certain common triggers can be identified.

Some individuals possess an innate, heightened sense of intuition from birth, often extending to the ability to perceive spirits. While this capability may manifest in childhood, individuals tend to suppress it as they mature, only for a significant life event to reignite it unexpectedly.

For others, psychic awakening occurs due to specific life incidents, frequently tinged with tragedy, such as accidents or near-death experiences. Additionally, hypnosis emerges as a potential trigger, as healing sessions involving energy flow can induce shifts in awareness, leading to the revelation of psychic abilities.

The pivotal question is: how do you navigate this awakening? Will you embrace it, or will you stifle it? It is crucial to recognize that everyone is born with intuition, a "sixth sense." If you find yourself becoming more intuitive, do not panic; this is a natural progression. Notably, even esteemed and logical figures like Albert Einstein acknowledged the importance of intuition. The unfamiliarity and strangeness associated with the awakening phase are part of the process and pose no cause for fear.

THE SIGNIFICANT MOTIVATIONS TO EMBRACE YOUR INNATE TALENT

Analogously to how parents encourage their children to develop hidden talents, investing time and effort to ensure proper training, what if the concealed talent encompasses an extraordinary gift like psychic ability? The nurturing of such hidden potential can lead to its blossoming into something truly extraordinary.

Consider psychic ability as an exceptional skill that, when further developed, possesses the potential to wield considerable influence, potentially making a positive impact on the world. This compelling reason underscores the importance of seizing the opportunity to cultivate your innate psychic gift: the ability to aid others in ways beyond imagination. The following are some compelling reasons that should persuade you to explore and develop your unique gift.

8

Understanding and Embracing Your Gift

Not everyone may label their empathic traits as a gift, and at times, these qualities may seem more like a burden than a blessing. Nevertheless, it is crucial to cultivate a mindset that perceives your empathic abilities as a gift. By comprehending and accepting the characteristics inherent in being an empath, you can leverage this unique gift to contribute to the healing of people globally. The extent to which you choose to utilize your gift and the manner in which you deploy it is entirely within your control. For example, you can employ it in a nonprofit organization dedicated to assisting individuals living in poverty. Alternatively, you might pursue a career as a counselor, aiding people through the most challenging phases of their lives. Your empathic abilities could also be employed to propagate compassion worldwide, whether by traveling to support those affected by natural disasters, participating in initiatives like Habitat for Humanity, or establishing your own charitable organization.

Attributes of an Empath

After completing a brief questionnaire to identify empathic characteristics, it's time to delve deeper into understanding these traits. It's crucial to recognize that not all empaths share identical characteristics, and certain aspects may be more pronounced than others. For instance, an empath may find themselves more attuned to others' emotional states rather than their physical well-being. Having one characteristic without the presence of another doesn't negate one's empathic nature.

Moreover, the level of awareness and attunement to their empathic abilities varies among individuals. Newly discovered empaths may not fully comprehend their capabilities, impacting the intensity with which they perceive others' emotions or sense the prevailing mood upon entering a room.

While there are numerous characteristics associated with empaths, the primary ones encompass:

1. **Intuition for Deception:** Empaths possess an often overlooked ability to discern when someone is lying. This may manifest as an instinctive feeling or an unsettling sensation caused by the discrepancy between spoken words and genuine emotions. Empaths may also simply think and recognize that someone is being untruthful.

2. **Sensitivity to Emotions and Physical Ailments:** A hallmark sign of being an empath is the ability to sense others' emotions. Whether through conversation, proximity, or merely sharing a space, empaths can discern feelings such as sadness, joy, frustration, or fear. This sensitivity extends to perceiving physical ailments, such as stomachaches or tension in the chest.

3. **Healing Powers:** Empaths often find people seeking their advice due to an inherent healing power that sets them apart. Though recipients may not explicitly acknowledge it, they invariably feel a positive shift after receiving guidance. Empaths can provide comfort and wisdom in unexpected situations, fostering a more optimistic outlook.

4. **Preemptive Awareness of Room Atmosphere:** Empaths who understand their gifts routinely pause to assess the atmosphere or energy of a room before entering. This practice allows them to shield themselves from external

negativity or mentally prepare for the emotional tenor awaiting them. For instance, if they sense an undercurrent of sadness, they anticipate discussions or news of a somber nature.

5. **High Sensitivity:** Empaths often fall under the category of highly sensitive individuals, frequently criticized for being "too sensitive." They easily experience emotional hurt, yet their nurturing disposition, spiritual openness, non-judgmental nature, and attentive listening skills make them exceptional caretakers.

6. **Introversion:** Empaths typically lean towards introversion, requiring ample time alone. Being introverted, in this context, doesn't necessarily equate to shyness or social aversion but implies a preference for internal contemplation. Introverted empaths focus on their inner thoughts and emotions, necessitating solitary moments for balance.

7. **Overextending for Others:** Empaths commonly prioritize others' feelings over their own, often neglecting self-care. Feeling a responsibility to utilize their healing abilities for the well-being of others, empaths must recognize the importance of maintaining their emotional, mental, and physical health to effectively aid those around them.

Experiencing violence, whether through television or online content, is a challenging ordeal for empaths who possess heightened sensitivity. If you're someone who instinctively changes channels or closes videos at the sight of violence, you likely fall into the empath category. The intense reactions, such as stomach-churning and potential physical illness, stem from this heightened sensitivity. However, it's often difficult for others to comprehend this sensitivity, leading to judgment or confusion when you abruptly leave a room or shield yourself from violent imagery.

Consider a scenario where you're engrossed in a documentary about the Ku Klux Klan, showing historical footage of violence against African Americans.

Overwhelmed by the graphic content, you decide to leave the room, despite your interest in the documentary. Friends may question your reaction, asserting that it's an essential part of history. Despite external opinions, empaths grapple with guilt about avoiding violent situations, recognizing that their mental and emotional well-being takes precedence.

In relationships, empaths face distinct challenges. Whether friendships, romantic entanglements, or marriages, sustaining these connections demands considerable effort. Intimate relationships pose a unique struggle for empaths, who keenly perceive shifts in their partner's mood and detect underlying issues. Even if external stressors cause changes in behavior, the emotional impact on empaths remains profound. Empaths may find their homes, which were once sanctuaries, becoming spaces shared with others, leading to overwhelming feelings and a lack of personal space.

While navigating intimate relationships, empaths must strike a balance to preserve their well-being. Open communication with partners becomes crucial to achieving a harmonious coexistence. Finding time for solitude becomes even more challenging, especially with the presence of younger children. However, by openly discussing and negotiating alone time with your significant other, a healthy and happy lifestyle can be maintained. Understandably, not every day will be perfect, and some days may necessitate more extended breaks. The key lies in overcoming guilt associated with taking time for oneself, recognizing its importance in maintaining a strong psychological balance.

9

Normalizing and Maintaining Your Gift

Irrespective of our capacity for empathy or the lack thereof, the common goal for everyone is to infuse their lives with as much joy as possible. Empaths, in particular, should notice an overall increase in their happiness levels as they become adept at identifying and managing various energies surrounding them. This proficiency enables them to make consistently positive choices by being more discerning.

However, even for those who master these skills and dedicate their energy to positivity, achieving constant and everlasting joy is an impractical objective. Everyone possesses blind spots, vulnerabilities, and weaknesses. Sooner or later, empowered empaths may confront a source of negativity that they cannot, or choose not to, overlook, compartmentalize, or resolve.

During such moments when joy seems unattainable, empaths must learn to seek inner peace instead. Consider the scenario where someone deeply loved and respected has passed away. Expecting anyone, even an empowered empath, to find true joy during funeral services or within the mourning period is unreasonable. Regardless of one's beliefs about death and the afterlife, a loss of this magnitude is always painful.

If an empath decides to attend a wake or funeral, they must prepare themselves for the experience, employing necessary strategies to avoid absorbing the pain of other mourners. However, an empath solely focused on pursuing joy risks neglecting genuine feelings of pain, thereby disconnecting from emotions that are uniquely their own. This practice is perilous for any empath to adopt, as it may initially seem alluring. Similar to an alcoholic attempting to evade the aftermath of a hangover by consistently consuming more alcohol, empaths will realize they cannot outrun their own emotions, even if they attempt to shut them out as they do with negative feelings from others.

Ultimately, the superior goal is balance. An empath with a strong sense of inner balance can attend a funeral, empathize with others, honor their sadness, and process feelings of grief without being overwhelmed. Their equilibrium allows them to understand that sorrow is not an opposing force to happiness but rather a functional part of joy. Without experiencing misery, one would never truly feel bliss or perhaps any emotion at all.

Over time, empaths will discover that this state of equilibrium represents their most heightened state of being, the place where they find their authentic selves.

Embrace Discomfort

Here's a groundbreaking concept that can elevate your yoga, tai chi, or mindfulness practice: discomfort is merely an emotion. It's not tangible; it poses no real threat, yet it serves as a catalyst for motivation.

Embracing discomfort differs from desensitizing oneself to it. When you acknowledge cognitive dissonance or moral injustices, numbing yourself to discomfort leads to apathy, fostering a distortion of truth. However, allowing discomfort without immediate reaction enables you to make empowered choices, conquer fears and anxieties, and progress emotionally. For empaths, discomfort often manifests as uncertainty or anticipation of conflict. By recognizing this feeling without triggering a fight-or-flight response, you can focus on constructive action, becoming the true master of your universe.

This enlightened stance is rare among humans. By using discomfort as a tool instead of avoiding it, you may find the ability to overcome challenges that would leave others defeated. Once you've mastered this technique, consider paying it forward to another empath.

Live an Authentic Life

A lack of authenticity in lifestyle can disrupt an empath's inner peace. Empaths may carry lies or dishonesty, haunted by them and allowing these memories to block their throat, heart, and solar plexus chakras. Hence, empaths should minimize lying, even avoiding white lies, as they can disrupt the energy field.

Strive for authenticity through both addition and elimination. Invite positive energy flow by aligning career, relationships, eating habits, and hobbies with your values. For instance, if environmentalism is crucial to you, working in green planning and connecting with like-minded individuals can be a significant step. Eliminate anything causing moral conflict, such as jobs or relationships that don't align with your values.

Stop supporting brands with conflicting values and quit habits negatively impacting what matters most to you. Be cautious with social media use, using it sparingly and posting honestly and responsibly.

Choosing Humility and Respecting the Unknown

Regardless of empowerment and empathic abilities, it's crucial to embrace humility and remain open to unexpected possibilities. A self-righteous empath with a narrow worldview may struggle with communication and relationships, appearing arrogant and standoffish.

Truth is multifaceted and always changing. To grasp even a sliver of it, an empath must maintain a balanced connection between their interior and exterior worlds. Shutting either out will lead to misleading messages or misinterpretations.

Empaths have unique knowledge but can occasionally be wrong, especially with limited external information. The ancient Indian parable of blind men encountering an elephant emphasizes the importance of acknowledging diverse perspectives.

Human nature tends to resist evolving past fixed vantage points, but the empath's enlightenment lies in gathering contrasting perspectives and incorporating them into a comprehensive philosophy. This requires staying humble and open to uncomfortable experiences.

While avoiding decisively negative energy, the empath should not shy away from challenging and unpredictable opportunities. Continuous growth involves trying new things, meeting new people, and seeking challenges. The universe has much more to teach the empath, and expanding one's perspective is crucial for growth.

10

Trust Your Intuition

Within your mind, a subtle inner voice, a tingling sensation, an instinctual urge – these are the messages conveyed by your gut feelings. It prompts the question: what message do they convey, and is it imperative to heed their advice? Many of us have encountered instances where we sense knowledge before it becomes apparent. For instance, you pause at a green traffic light, narrowly avoiding a collision with a car that ran a red light. Or, you spontaneously decide to embark on a blind date, only to discover the love of your life.

If we could tap into these intuitive insights more effectively, our decision-making could be enhanced. The good news is that we have the capacity to do so, provided we learn to recognize and interpret the signals. These signals may manifest as butterflies in your stomach, a strong conviction that an event is imminent, or clammy palms.

Contrary to its elusive nature, intuition possesses a tangible aspect. The intuitive right hemisphere of the brain observes your surroundings while the left hemisphere is preoccupied with other tasks. The body registers this information even when the conscious mind remains oblivious to the ongoing processes.

According to a theoretical perspective, the anticipation of an upcoming event might be attributed to dopamine neurons. Dopamine functions as a vigilant tracker of reality, alerting us to patterns that elude conscious detection.

The challenge lies in discerning which gut feeling to trust. It involves striking a delicate balance between intuition and rational thinking, combining the insights from both the mind and the gut instinct. When an intuitive impression arises, engaging the mind to evaluate options and determine a course of action becomes crucial.

Consider These Intuitive Signals

That Experts Suggest You Take Notice Of:

Sensing Discomfort in Your Body

Being attuned to your body's cues is an essential aspect of honing your intuitive instincts. Your body serves as an effective communicator, providing early warnings when something isn't right. Intuition can guide you to address issues promptly. If you sense toxicity or weakness, heed the intuition and seek attention. Many individuals overlook these signals, only to discover that minor concerns escalate into major problems.

Physical symptoms often carry symbolic significance. If your energy drops when near someone, don't dismiss this intuition. Fatigue may indicate exposure to an energy-draining environment or person. Your body might be signaling that these conditions are depleting your energy, potentially leading to feelings of being stuck, anxious, or depressed.

Take note of sudden physical sensations during interactions. For instance, a burning stomach sensation might precede a decision not to take a cab, later discovering the driver's arrest for theft. Intuitions can manifest in various parts of your body, with the stomach being a common site due to housing the enteric nervous system, often referred to as the second brain.

Feeling Threatened

The instinctual feelings you experience within the first ten seconds of meeting someone stem from ancient biological wisdom. Early humans who could swiftly distinguish between friend and foe had a higher survival rate. Modern descendants retain the ability to instantly interpret emotional signals from others.

While social conditioning can shape beliefs, leading to flawed impressions and decisions, it's advisable to cross-check gut feelings with rational thinking. When feeling uneasy or unable to trust someone, pay attention to those instincts. If walking alone, and a person approaching raises concern, consider changing your path or crossing the street.

Desire to Assist

Our gut instincts evolved to help us avoid danger, but our heightened evolution allows us to sense when a friend needs help. Sympathy is ingrained, prompting our brains to consider others' feelings. Evolution equipped us to read faces and signals, empowering us to offer help without waiting to be asked. Even small gestures can significantly impact someone's day, and generosity triggers the brain's pleasure center, benefiting overall well-being, immunity, and mood.

Trusting Your Expertise

There are tasks you may struggle with, even if you've done them countless times. Familiar actions may become challenging when overthinking comes into play. The innate ability to tackle challenges gets drowned out by excessive analysis.

For beginners, rational thinking aids in developing technique and muscle memory. However, experienced individuals perform better when relying on instincts, as overthinking disrupts established neural patterns. When tempted to overanalyze tasks, distraction, such as reciting the alphabet backward or singing a favorite song, can free up your instincts to perform effectively.

This Feels Appropriate

When your intuition signals that a person or situation is right for you, the decision becomes effortless. It feels natural, without any sense of force.

When faced with significant decisions carrying lasting repercussions, trust your gut. Relying on gut instincts for major choices leads to more satisfying outcomes, ultimately enhancing your quality of life.

Explore and Trust Your Intuition through these Practices

Unearthing and relying on your intuition involves breaking free from ingrained beliefs and embracing self-discovery. Our core beliefs, shaped since birth, evolve with experiences and circumstances, often attempting to control us like an unwavering alter ego. To overcome this, reflect on self-perceptions, navigate through negativity, and acknowledge your journey, paving the way to trust your intuition.

Release the Shackles of Childhood

Childhood memories, both positive and negative, shape our understanding of the world. Growing older brings an awareness of the challenges faced by our parents. To trust your intuition, appreciate and forgive, avoiding blame for adult choices on childhood experiences. Holding onto childhood hurts impedes progress and hinders intuitive trust.

Heed the Inner Voice

Listening to your gut requires acknowledging the subtle voice within your heart or mind. Although seemingly straightforward, some may need time to develop this skill. Resist self-doubt, reflect on past instances where ignoring your instincts led to unfavorable outcomes, and recognize that trusting your gut is a reliable guide.

Meditate Anywhere

Meditation, whether walking outdoors, quietly on a cushion, or in unexpected places like a subway or doctor's office, offers a chance to find tranquility between thoughts. This quiet space nurtures compassion, clarity, and self-understanding, fostering a safe environment to connect with your intuition. Regular meditation keeps your intuitive senses fresh.

Forgive Self-Harm
Recognize and break free from forms of self-harm, such as excessive drinking or isolation, driven by the belief of unworthiness. Replace self-punishment with forgiveness and compassion, filling the void with mindfulness and love.

Release Resentments and Attachments
Letting go of attachments and resentments clears space for personal growth. Holding onto negative feelings only allows them to fester. By releasing these emotional bonds, you create room to trust yourself and rely on your intuition.

Return to Self
Avoid the habit of compulsively seeking distractions. Instead, embrace self-discovery and connect with your inner self. Trusting yourself leads to feeling secure in the world, promoting attentiveness to your intuition.

Embrace Imperfection
Recognize that everyone is a work in progress, requiring practice, patience, and willingness to embark on the journey of self-discovery. Awakening and connecting with your intuition opens the door to endless possibilities.

Personal Meditation Techniques
Enhance your connection with your divine and higher self through personalized meditation practices. Strengthening this connection makes trusting your intuition more natural.

Sleep Meditation Routine
Customize the length of this meditation to suit your needs. Repeat as

necessary to ease into sleep, fostering a deeper connection with yourself.

Laughter Meditation Challenge

An advanced practice involving stretching, laughter, and stillness. Allocate approximately 12 minutes, preferably in the morning on an empty stomach, to reap the benefits of this transformative meditation. If the morning doesn't suit you, try before lunch or dinner.

Begin with body stretching, interlocking your fingers and raising your arms with palms facing up. Slowly release tension, embracing the laughter and subsequent stillness that follows.

11

Types of Empaths

Upon comprehending the aforementioned traits, you can now determine whether you possess empathic qualities. If you do, the subsequent section will elaborate on the specific type of empath you might be. However, it is essential to acknowledge two commonalities among all empaths. Firstly, every empath is inherently endowed with the capacity to perceive and share the experiences of others, whether through emotions or sensations. Secondly, empaths are not inherently skilled; they must acquire and refine their abilities, as lacking these skills can lead to distress. If you currently lack these skills, rest assured, as this book is designed to aid you in acquiring the necessary empathic skills. Interestingly, you might discover that you embody multiple empathic types, often referred to as the diverse gifts of empathy.

Physical Intuition – The second empathic category involves physical or medical empathy. If you possess this form of empathy, you can discern another person's physical health and well-being. Similar to emotional empaths, you tap into the experience, but instead of emotions, you connect with their physiological state. This may manifest as receiving images or a sense of something amiss. For instance, if someone has a chronic illness like diabetes, the term 'diabetes' might inexplicably appear in your mind. Alternatively, you may sense another person's symptoms, akin to how emotional empaths perceive emotions. This can be disconcerting if not understood, leading to experiencing numerous symptoms daily despite being in good health. Some physical/medical empaths can even identify energy issues in others, such as blockages or imbalances, making practices like Reiki beneficial for them. Many choose medical professions, utilizing their intuition to diagnose and treat patients.

Physical Oneness – These empaths receive information on a personal level. They feel the physical state of others in their own bodies when in close proximity. For instance, when with someone like Betty, a physical oneness empath might develop a stomachache, as if it belongs to Betty. Although this type may seem perplexing, a skilled individual can use this ability to assist others, provided they navigate it with expertise to avoid confusion or suffering.

Intuitive Empath – This category involves individuals who gather information about others simply by spending time with them. They can discern a person's nature and characteristics intuitively, often being mistaken for psychics or mind readers due to their ability to pick up on cues effectively. These empaths are highly attuned to the energy around them, allowing them to deduce what is transpiring in the minds of others. Being an intuitive empath may enable you to perceive aspects about someone, such as their role as a parent or their current challenges, solely through spending time with them. Unlike emotional empaths, they don't need verbal communication to understand others, relying on their intuitive insights. However, they may find large crowds overwhelming, as constant absorption of information from the surroundings can be intense.

Intellectual Empath Ability – This empathic type has the ability to tap into people's intellectual capacities. For instance, they may find themselves using complex vocabulary when conversing with someone like Joy, only later realizing that Joy also has a penchant for using intricate language.

Emotional Sensitivity – The most prevalent and fundamental type of empath is the emotional empath. It is the variation that typically comes to mind when people think of empaths. As an emotional empath, you possess the ability to perceive the emotions of those around you, gaining insight into a person's feelings regardless of their outward expressions. While this heightened sensitivity can be a valuable asset, allowing you to truly understand others, it can also pose challenges. Distinguishing between your own emotions and those of others becomes a complex task, leading to emotional confusion.

Describing your ability merely as sensing others' emotions might downplay your experience. In reality, you not only sense but also share in those emotions. This shared emotional experience may result in mood swings, making you appear emotionally unstable at times. Therefore, it becomes crucial to develop the skill of distinguishing between others' emotions and your own, ensuring authenticity in your emotional state across various environments. Maintaining emotional detachment proves advantageous, especially when aiding others, as it prevents your energies from being altered or drained by their emotional experiences.

These empaths possess the capability to discern what is transpiring in someone's emotional realm, even when efforts are made to conceal or feign those emotions. For example, an empath might detect that Betty, seemingly always cheerful, is concealing worries behind her smiles. Proficient empaths excel at differentiating between genuine and fake emotions, enhancing their ability to be supportive friends who truly understand those around them.

Emotional Unity – This empathic type involves delving into the true essence of others' emotions. Unlike Emotional Intuition, emotional unity allows an empath to not only sense but also feel what others are experiencing. Emotions tend to intertwine between you and your friends. A skilled empath must navigate absorbing predominantly negative emotions without being overwhelmed, assisting friends in overcoming such negativity, whether it be worries or anger. Skill in emotional unity involves maintaining a stable emotional foundation to offer effective support.

Spiritual Sensitivity – This empathic category entails experiencing how others connect with a higher power or spiritual entities. For instance, accompanying Betty to church provides insight into the spiritual flavor she derives from her pastor's teachings about God. This connection can unfold even when unaware of your friend's religious views. Skilled empaths leverage this opportunity to explore diverse aspects of spirituality, fostering an interest in various religions.

Spiritual Unity – Differing from Spiritual Sensitivity, Spiritual Unity involves directly experiencing how friends connect with their Supreme Being. This connection may manifest through hymns, allowing skilled empaths to deepen their spiritual growth.

Animal Empathy – An animal empath perceives what it feels like to inhabit the consciousness of a specific animal. Unlike animal lovers, skilled animal empaths can discern differences between seemingly identical animals, assisting them in locating their groups or aiding pet owners. These empaths, often found in the company of animal companions, dedicate their lives to caring for animals through various roles such as pet ownership, running pet stores, working in shelters, or contributing to animal sanctuaries.

Environmental Empathy – Environmental empaths possess the ability to distinguish between landscapes in different environments, finding emotional resonance in each setting.

Plant Empathy – Plant empaths experience the sensations of being a particular tree, leaf, or flower. Skilled empaths channel this gift into agriculture or gardening.

Crystal Sensitivity – Crystal empaths connect with the consciousness of specific gemstones or crystals, gaining information and inspiration by surrounding themselves with these stones.

Mechanical Sensitivity – Mechanical empaths understand what it feels like to be a specific machine and comprehend its needs. This understanding empowers skilled empaths to diagnose and fix machines without formal qualifications, sparking a heightened interest in machinery and technology.

12

Empath and Relationsh

In your personal life, you wield more influence than you might realize. The relationships you cultivate have a deliberate purpose—whether to facilitate personal growth, deepen self-awareness, or provide nurturing support. Each relationship essentially serves as a kind of "test," requiring you to comprehend its nature and understand its current impact on your life.

Should you find relationships geared towards your growth and self-discovery, they may vary in positivity or negativity. Positive instances may involve friendships with fellow empaths, guiding you to understand your potential and encouraging the development of your innate gifts. Conversely, negative relationships may reveal your weaknesses, indicating where you lack self-care and firm boundaries. In such cases, these relationships become opportunities to recognize how others may exploit or harm you, prompting you to be more present and available for yourself. By navigating these negative relationships, setting clear boundaries, and prioritizing self-care, some may naturally evolve into healthier connections, offering a more enjoyable and secure environment. On the other hand, some may become increasingly toxic, necessitating the termination of the relationship to break free from its harmful elements—an important lesson for empaths.

Relationships designed to provide support and a safe space for self-expression are inherently positive and should be nurtured. These connections contribute to your understanding of the value of strong relationships and your own self-worth. Generally, minimal intervention is required in such relationships, except possibly clarifying new boundaries if needed. Often, boundary violations occur not out of disrespect but due to the lack of awareness. Asserting your boundaries can lead to immediate positive shifts in behavior, with individuals honoring and celebrating your commitment to self-respect.

While love often demands vulnerability, the experience is heightened for sensitive individuals. Highly sensitive people (HSPs) may find relationships challenging due to their heightened awareness of their surroundings and the people they engage with. This increased sensitivity may lead to stress and a need for more downtime, potentially straining relationships. Despite these challenges, many are drawn to HSPs for their openness, compassion, empathy, and authentic approach to life.

Highly sensitive individuals often attract those in need, but this attraction can be misleading, leading them into relationships where their caring nature is exploited. Unfortunately, this can result in HSPs becoming the doormats of their social circles, seeking therapy to cope with the consequences. The lack of acceptance for their sensitivity can cause HSPs to suffer from low self-esteem and self-doubt, impacting their romantic relationships. HSPs, in their pursuit of love and acceptance, tend to become more helpful, empathetic, compassionate, and attuned to the needs and feelings of others.

Mate sensitivity, a distinctive trait of HSPs, involves quickly deciphering a partner's needs and proactively addressing issues to restore happiness. While this trait is admirable, problems may arise when one party gives excessively. The imbalance of giving without reciprocation leads to unmet needs, leaving the giver feeling unhappy, resentful, and exhausted. In such situations, blame is often directed inward, further contributing to unfulfillment.

Ways for Highly Sensitive Persons (HSPs) to Enhance Relationship Satisfaction

Establishing contentment in relationships can pose challenges for highly sensitive individuals. Nevertheless, the ensuing recommendations can assist HSPs in fostering greater satisfaction within their relationships:

1. Allocate Personal Time:

Balancing the need for a fulfilling relationship with the requirement for personal downtime is crucial for HSPs. Striking a harmonious equilibrium between spending quality time with a partner and retreating for personal space is essential. Failure to unwind and carve out moments alone can lead to overstimulation, resulting in issues like anxiety, depression, frustration, and burnout. To find this balance, cultivate a consistent routine that allows for both shared moments and personal solitude.

2. Embrace Direct Communication:

To ensure your needs are met reciprocally, HSPs must adopt a more direct communication approach. While HSPs possess intuitive abilities that enable them to anticipate others' needs easily, non-HSP partners may lack similar awareness. Expecting equal care and consideration may lead to disappointment, as non-HSP individuals might not grasp these needs inherently. Express your desires clearly, adjusting your communication style to ensure your needs are effectively communicated.

3. Take Breaks During Conflict:

Conflicts can be challenging for HSPs, triggering overstimulation and a fight-or-flight response. Instead of succumbing to this reaction, take a breather during conflicts. Allow emotions to subside and collaboratively develop strategies for managing conflict. Establish rules for communication, breaks, and expressing needs, fostering an environment where both HSP and non-HSP partners can navigate conflicts with ease.

4. Accept Differences:

Recognize that conflicts often arise from individual disparities, including differences in empathy, sensitivity, and emotional responsiveness. Regardless of HSP status, acknowledge the existence of varying sensitivities and preferences between partners.

5. Cultivate Intentional Connections through Shared Experiences:

Combatting feelings of neglect and conflict requires actively connecting with others. Amidst life's distractions, prioritize quality time with your partner. Engage in activities that foster communication and understanding, delving into deeper levels of knowledge about each other's likes, dislikes, aspirations, and challenges. Building intimate connections lays the foundation for enduring relationships.

6. Celebrate Achievements:

Counteract the human tendency towards a negativity bias by celebrating successes. As an HSP, focus on the positive aspects within and around you. Acknowledge achievements, as dwelling on difficulties can exacerbate negative emotions and impact physical and emotional well-being. Recognizing and celebrating successes contributes to a more positive relationship experience for HSPs.

13

Tips for Empathsin Intimate Relationship

1. Incorporate some personal time into your daily routine, even if it's just a brief break – perhaps five or ten minutes for a walk or journaling. Reserve an hour each week for dedicated self-care, whether that involves a relaxing bath, meditation, yoga, a nature hike, or quality time with your pet.

2. Maintain transparency with your partner. If you require extra alone time, communicate this clearly. For instance, after a day filled with handshakes and meetings, you might need to sleep alone. Reassure your partner that it's about self-care and not a reflection on them; a supportive partner will understand.

3. Encourage open communication with your partner about their needs. In times of crisis, you want them to feel comfortable sharing their requirements, allowing for compromises like sacrificing personal time one day or extending quality time over the weekend.

4. If you share a living space, designate an area solely for yourself, whether it's a "she-shed," "man-cave," or any space you can call your own. Even if you share a bed regularly, having a personal retreat, whether it's a garden, patio, or a converted closet, can be beneficial. Ensure it's a space where you feel comfortable, and unless it's an emergency, limit visitors to your pet.

5. Prioritize your feelings in the relationship. Speak up and express your opinions, even if they differ from your partner's. If you're empathetic, fear of losing your identity in the relationship may be a concern. Remember that you have the power to prevent that. Your partner loves you for who you are, not as an extension of themselves. If they seek an extension, it may be time to consider a more suitable partner.

Overcoming the fear of closeness holds significant importance. Love plays a vital role in our lives, and your unique abilities empower you to feel its depth more intensely than the average individual. Being cherished by an empath is a fortunate circumstance. When selecting a partner for an intimate connection, it's crucial to steer clear of individuals with energy-draining tendencies, as they are naturally drawn to empaths like yourself.

Navigating a Close Connection with an Empath

Are you aware if your significant other identifies as an empath, or is it a possibility you're considering? If your partner isn't cognizant of their empathic nature, initiate a conversation. Suggest they engage in the "Am I an Empath?" exercise to explore this aspect of themselves.

Being in an intimate relationship with an empath promises an abundance of love and compassion, but it may also entail nights of solitude and a preference for home over social gatherings. Empaths require alone time to decompress, and sometimes physical touch or mere proximity can be overwhelming. Assess whether the positives of being with your empathic partner outweigh the challenges.

If you find that being with an empath is challenging, part ways respectfully and compassionately. Avoid placing blame if you can't cope with the time your partner needs alone; instead, be honest about your needs. Understand that you both have different requirements that may not be reconcilable.

Prepare to sacrifice some privacy, as empaths naturally pick up on emotions and absorb energy. Don't expect them to maintain emotional shields at all times, especially at home, where they should feel at ease. Encourage self-care for both you and your partner, exploring activities like organic, raw food diets, yoga, or meditation. Embrace silence and practice mindfulness during shared activities.

Honesty is crucial with empaths; attempting to deceive them is futile. They possess an innate ability to discern emotions, even if they are not explicitly claircognizant or intuitive empaths. Respect their sensitivity to body language and avoid dishonesty.

If your partner is an animal empath, acknowledge their unique bond with their pet. Be prepared for the presence of fur on your clothes and refrain from asking them to choose between you and their pet. Understand that it's an unfair request, and the answer may not be to your liking.

Recognize that empaths are sensitive and prone to hurt feelings, which they cannot control. Take responsibility for managing your reactions during disagreements. Approach arguments with compassion, focusing on improving the relationship rather than determining who is right or wrong.

Support your partner in establishing boundaries and cutting out energy vampires from their life. Assist them in maintaining these boundaries for a healthier, happier partnership. Be understanding when they feel guilty about setting boundaries and explain the importance of doing so. If a friend is perceived as an energy vampire, socialize with them outside the home.

Acknowledge and respect your partner's need for boundaries, even with you. Empaths will always require some time and space to be alone, irrespective of your closeness. Encourage the creation of a personal space at home for them to retreat and decompress. Resist the temptation to snoop when they're not around.

While it's easy to become complacent in a relationship with an empath, reciprocate their love and support to ensure its thriving. Initiate conversations about their empathic experiences, demonstrating an open mind and acceptance. Counter any feelings of weirdness or shame they may have about their abilities, affirming your acceptance of them exactly as they are. Express your needs honestly, emphasizing the importance of compromise in maintaining a balanced relationship.

14

Tools for Transformation and Spiritual Growth

Some individuals regret being empaths, particularly when they've invested a great deal of emotion in someone only to have their feelings shattered. Navigating life as an empath can be challenging, especially if one hasn't acknowledged their empathic nature or honed their abilities. Experiencing exploitation or profound hurt is never enjoyable. The initial step involves introspection, understanding what defines one's empathic qualities, and finding constructive ways to leverage these abilities.

Each empath is unique, with no universal mold. Uniqueness is a defining trait, as we are individuals with a profound connection to the feelings and experiences of those around us. Our purpose revolves around aiding and healing others in diverse ways. While the instinct is to catch others when they fall, it's crucial to prioritize personal well-being. The analogy of the airplane safety procedure applies – securing your own mask before assisting others. Taking care of oneself first ensures the ability to provide assistance and healing to others later on.

Empaths and the Process of Spiritual Awakening

It is often said that everyone begins as empaths, but over time, many lose the ability to attune to the emotions of others. Immunity to feelings becomes commonplace. A spiritual awakening, however, acts as a catalyst, rekindling an awareness of our own emotions and kickstarting a journey of introspection. This reawakening marks the restoration of our capacity to scrutinize our internal workings.

The spiritual awakening process manifests in various forms, typically unfolding through seven distinct stages:

1. Experience of unhappiness and emptiness.
2. A shift in perspective.
3. Quest for answers and meaning.
4. Discovery of solutions and breakthroughs.
5. Period of feeling lost once again.
6. Delving into analysis and profound inner work.
7. Attainment of joy through integration and expansion.

The initial stage of unhappiness and emptiness often arises from a significant life event, whether it be a crisis, divorce, trauma, death, illness, or another transformative occurrence. During this phase, individuals may unknowingly isolate themselves from the world, exacerbating their struggles.

The subsequent change in perspective involves a heightened awareness, where one begins to discern the falsehoods present in their surroundings. Feelings of discontent and occasional anger or sadness may resemble a roller coaster of emotions, indicative of the mind processing the unfolding reality.

As seekers progress, they enter a phase of questioning and searching for meaning. Whether grappling with the aftermath of betrayal or another life-altering event, individuals embark on a quest to understand and rectify their situations, delving into extensive research.

Upon finding mentors and resources that provide answers to their inquiries, individuals experience breakthroughs and moments of enlightenment, leading to a renewed sense of joy and happiness.

The journey, however, is not without its ups and downs. Periods of feeling lost prompt seekers to seek further knowledge, exploring connections with others and seeking deeper meanings, often fueled by a sense of boredom with the self or current mentors.

The stage of analysis and deep inner work becomes pivotal, as individuals rely on themselves to alleviate any lingering pain. Grounding practices, such as various forms of meditation, take precedence as a means to reconnect with oneself and find inner peace.

These stages collectively constitute a common path toward spiritual awakening, though some may recognize this transformation, while others may not. Five signs indicative of a spiritual awakening include avoiding negative influences, heightened intuition, increased inner peace, a surge of positivity and compassion, and an enhancement of authenticity.

You steer clear of individuals with a negative demeanor. If someone engages in gossip, judgment, or other dramatic behavior, you tend to distance yourself from such individuals. You reach a point where you find such behavior trivial.

Your intuition has heightened. Rather than merely listening to what people say, you focus more on their actions, recognizing that actions speak louder than words. It's crucial to be observant and not rely solely on someone's word, as manipulative individuals may attempt to alter the narrative.

Inner peace has grown within you. Seeking validation becomes unnecessary, and you develop a preference for quiet and alone time. Social media takes a back seat in your life, and you realize there's no need to measure your worth by the number of likes on a post; contentment arises from within.

A surge of positivity and compassion envelops you. Instead of wishing for others to fail, you find yourself wanting to uplift them. Recognizing our shared struggles and connections, you genuinely wish everyone the best.

Authenticity is accentuated. Rather than seeking the spotlight, you prefer to take a back seat and allow others to shine. Your need for attention in crowds or social gatherings diminishes, and you may even feel apprehensive if the focus is on you.

Experiencing a spiritual awakening can be profound. It has the potential to catalyze transformative shifts in life, happiness, health, and abundance at a rapid pace. While not always easy to navigate, a spiritual awakening permanently enriches your life. Once you navigate the challenges, you'll appreciate the incredible nature of the experience and never want to let it go.

15

Your Guide to Healing Meditation

For many individuals, the notion or concept of meditation can be unsettling at best and bothersome at worst. Are you someone who feels uneasy about the idea of meditating? Many individuals believe they lack the ability to sit still or claim they have insufficient time to incorporate meditation into their lives. Perhaps you believe it's an activity reserved only for Buddhists or those with ultra-spiritual inclinations. However, meditation is accessible to anyone seeking to enhance their mental well-being. It is suitable for people from all walks of life, and everyone, especially empaths, should consider integrating it into their routine. Before delving further, let's explore some precise definitions of meditation to help you become more at ease with what it involves.

Defining Meditation:

To begin with, let's explore the concept of meditation. It involves the practice of training and disciplining the mind. While this might appear somewhat abstract, it is, in reality, a straightforward and more accessible process than it may initially sound.

Transcendental Meditation:

One of the most well-known and widely practiced forms of meditation in the United States is Transcendental Meditation. Detailed information about this technique can be found online.

Kundalini Meditation:

Another approach is Kundalini meditation, which incorporates breathwork, mantras, physical movements, and hand signs (mudras). It's important to note that participation in meditation is not exclusive to yoga enthusiasts.

Mantra:

Mantras, comprising phrases or words repeated during meditation, serve to focus the mind on a specific intention or to achieve a state of silence. While not mandatory, some may find mantras helpful. For those curious about this method, listening to mantra chants on platforms like YouTube can provide insight.

The Miraculous Benefits of Regular Meditation:

Engaging in daily meditation can positively impact your health, happiness, and overall well-being. It has the potential to enhance health, alleviate fears, and improve intuition and emotional management.

You Can Embrace Meditation Too:

As an empath, prioritizing this simple activity can heighten your connection and intuition. This uncomplicated guide aims to demystify the practice, offering steps to make sense of your empathic gift and prevent burnout or overwhelm in daily situations.

Your Guide to Empath Healing Meditation:

Similar to acquiring any skill or adopting a practice, achieving results in meditation is possible with determination. Although starting meditation may seem challenging, it is more manageable than one might think. Commencing the practice requires a desire and willingness to enhance empathic abilities.

Setting Your Intention:

Initiating your meditation practice involves setting an intention. Reaffirming this intention daily, either aloud or in your mind, can infuse your practice with the enthusiasm and energy needed to persevere.

Recognize its Simplicity:

It's essential to understand that anyone can learn to meditate with the desire to do so.

Creating the Right Atmosphere:

Establish a dedicated meditation space in your home that is serene, uncluttered, and quiet. This space will be reserved exclusively for your meditation sessions. Keep in mind that meditation is adaptable to various environments over time.

Meditating Anywhere:

Although a quiet place is preferable when starting, meditation can eventually be practiced in different settings, such as in a car, during a bath, or on a train.

The Sacred Space:

Many meditation instructors emphasize the importance of creating a sacred space for meditation. Even in a small living space, lighting a candle and designating a specific pillow for meditation can contribute to this atmosphere.

Abandon the "No Time" Excuse:

Avoid telling yourself that you don't have time to meditate. Even if you can spare only 30 seconds or a minute, this brief period can help calm your mind and initiate meditation.

Start with a Minute:

For those resistant to the idea, try inhaling for five seconds, holding for five, exhaling for five, and repeating. Set a timer for one minute, gradually increasing by a minute each day. This gradual approach makes meditation more accessible and less daunting.

Discovering Serenity in the Rhythm of the Heartbeat

Embarking on meditation is as uncomplicated as redirecting your focus to your own pulse. This technique is particularly beneficial for meditation novices, fostering enhanced concentration and tranquility, even in the midst of the most challenging emotional states.

Seated Cross-Legged:
  Initiate the process by sitting on the floor with legs crossed.

Close the Eyes:
  Subsequently, close your eyes and center your thoughts on the space between your eyebrows.

Identify Your Objective:
  Contemplate your goal and transform it into a mantra, such as "I am intuitive and trust myself" or "I appreciate my empathic abilities."

Recite Your Mantra:
  Sync your chosen mantra with each heartbeat, repeating it rhythmically.

Advantages of this Effortless Approach:

This meditation method is available at any moment, providing substantial personal growth in just a few minutes daily. Consistent practice fosters a calm mind and nurtures your inner voice.

Internal Harmony Commences Here

The following technique is a Kundalini-style meditation, characterized by its effectiveness, simplicity, and swiftness. It can be performed anytime, anywhere.

Pressing Fingers Together:

Press your thumb against each finger sequentially.

Recite the Following:

As each finger is touched, vocalize the words "peace," "starts," "with," and "me."

Deep Breathing:

Simultaneously with the spoken words, inhale deeply at your preferred pace. This can be practiced on public transport, at your desk, or even during moments of disagreement.

Utilize this method to navigate through challenging emotional situations and release any harbored resentment.

Turning Your Commute into a Meditation

Public transportation provides an opportunity to meditate during your commute. Once seated on the bus or train, close your eyes and repeat a mantra.

This can be incorporated into your daily routine to and from work. You can either follow guided meditations or create your own steps.

Inhale and Exhale:
While commuting, synchronize your breath with the mantra or guided meditation. Breath control is fundamental to all meditation practices.

Focus on Positivity:
Concentrate on positive thoughts, such as your job competence or gratitude for life. Direct your attention to empowering sentiments.

Activity as a Meditation:

Any enjoyable activity can serve as a meditation, fostering detachment from thoughts and a sense of centeredness. Walking, in particular, is an excellent choice.

Walking Meditation:
Transform your walking routine into a meditation by breathing deeply with each step, feeling your feet, and repeating a mantra of calm and peace.

Incorporate this into your regular routine to reconnect with your empathic abilities, alleviate stress, and feel grounded.

Smart Technology Usage:

Contrary to the notion that technology induces stress, it can be a valuable tool for centering yourself and alleviating depression or anxiety.

Utilize Meditation Apps:
Download meditation apps, set meditation session timers, or explore affirmations online. Technology brought you to this book; remember to use it wisely.

Manage Online Time:

Reducing internet usage can diminish stress, fostering a calmer everyday life. Allocate time to more wholesome and creative activities instead of succumbing to social media distractions.

16

Empath Healing

Renouncing Destructive Empathetic Practices

If you identify as an empath, it's likely that you've developed certain tendencies that undermine your well-being and overall happiness. These tendencies aren't necessarily negative behaviors; rather, they often stem from positive traits without clear boundaries. Empaths, in their inclination to avoid saying "no," may find themselves overcommitting to the point where virtuous qualities like generosity and selflessness become overwhelming. It's crucial to identify and discard these practices to uphold emotional equilibrium, health, and general well-being. Key corrupt practices to relinquish include:

1. Persistent People-Pleasing: While aiming to please others is inherently positive, unchecked efforts can lead empaths to overextend themselves. Consistently saying "yes" may result in perpetual self-use, depriving you of the time needed to replenish energy levels. Prioritizing your own needs occasionally is a challenging yet essential lesson for empaths, as maintaining personal strength enables more effective assistance to others.

2. Enabling Behavior: Unlike the relatively benign act of trying to please others, enabling behavior is genuinely detrimental. Empaths may be inclined

to enable misbehavior due to their ability to empathize with the reasons behind it. However, enabling not only fails to help the other person but also harms the empath by perpetuating mistreatment. Recognizing and standing against harmful behavior, rather than enabling it, is essential for self-protection while still offering forgiveness and acceptance.

3. Carrying Others' Burdens: Empaths often feel compelled to alleviate others' suffering, sometimes by shouldering their burdens. While well-intentioned, this practice burdens empaths with more than they can handle and prevents individuals from learning life lessons from their consequences. Allowing others to experience their pains and burdens is crucial for personal growth.

4. Accepting Unwarranted Blame: The empathetic reluctance to harm others can lead to a tendency to accept blame even when not at fault. Continuously taking the blame prevents accountability for others' actions and hinders their learning process. Moreover, it burdens empaths with responsibility for others' actions and well-being, which can become overwhelming.

5. Obligatory Time Spending: Feeling obligated to spend time with others, while seemingly positive, can deplete valuable alone time essential for emotional recharging. Obligatory socializing may also expose empaths to negativity, leading to emotional fatigue and potential depression. Making choices that prioritize personal well-being is crucial for protection against emotional exhaustion.

6. Victim Mentality Addiction: Repeated victimization can lead empaths to identify with feelings of being drained, depressed, and taken advantage of. Breaking free from this ingrained perspective is essential, understanding that happiness and well-being are not exceptions but integral to one's purpose.

7. Energy Drainage for the Unappreciative: Providing time, effort, and emotional energy to those who take it for granted is a common way empaths fall victim. Letting go of those who do not appreciate your contributions

allows you to redirect your energy to those who value it, making your efforts more impactful.

8. Codependency: Sustaining a one-sided relationship where your energy is consistently taken without reciprocation can lead to constant depletion and depression. Empaths should prioritize mutually beneficial relationships, ending any one-sided connections to safeguard their happiness and peace of mind.

Best Practices to Begin

Establishing good practices is crucial for empaths to lead fulfilling lives. Simply identifying and addressing corrupt practices is only one part of the equation. The other vital aspect involves recognizing and adopting behaviors that contribute positively to one's well-being. Empaths bear an enhanced responsibility to safeguard and nurture their energies, necessitating the incorporation of practices conducive to maintaining health and happiness in any situation.

1. Acknowledge your empathic capabilities, a challenging task for many empaths. Understanding the perplexing and sometimes distressing nature of these abilities is pivotal. Acceptance aligns your mindset with your abilities, allowing you to hear and trust your inner voice, thereby resolving the inner conflicts frequently encountered by empaths.

2. Embracing your empathic gift is the subsequent step towards crafting a productive life. Nurturing these abilities is essential for personal improvement. Recognizing that empathic abilities are not solely for the benefit of others but also for personal growth is crucial. Learn to discern trustworthy individuals, utilizing your intuition to navigate paths leading to success and steering clear of failure.

3. Develop emotional detachment, a vital skill for empaths due to their

sensitivity. This mindset enables the recognition of others' emotions without being unduly affected. Practices such as meditation and mindfulness, endorsed by traditions like Buddhism, aid in emotional detachment, shielding empaths from the adverse effects of negative emotional environments.

4. Regular meditation proves to be an effective technique for cultivating emotional detachment. Finding a meditation method that suits individual preferences is key, as not all forms are alike. The chosen meditation practice not only fosters emotional detachment but also helps balance energies, releasing stress accumulated from exposure to negativity.

5. Engage in cathartic activities such as screaming, jumping, or intense exercise to alleviate stress and anxiety caused by negative energies. Physical exertion aids in burning off excess energy, and techniques like yelling or shouting provide a release of tension, restoring emotional strength, equilibrium, and harmony.

6. Foster somatic mindfulness to reconnect with your emotions amid the constant influx of external feelings. By focusing on different parts of your body, you can assess your emotional state. Tension in the jaw, elevated heart rate, shallow breathing, stiff shoulders, and clenched fists serve as indicators, helping you identify and address imbalances in your emotional well-being.

Maintaining a sense of grounding is a challenge for many empaths. One contributing factor is their tendency to overlook or misinterpret the signals indicating when they are ungrounded or emotionally unsteady. Furthermore, a lack of awareness regarding these signs exacerbates the issue. Another obstacle lies in the unfamiliarity with effective methods to regain balance and remain grounded even after recognizing these warning signs. Indications of being ungrounded encompass challenges in concentration and focus, reflective of emotional and mental fatigue that affects both empaths and individuals who aren't empaths. Empaths, however, may encounter this state more frequently, given the tendency for their emotional well-being to veer into chaos more regularly than that of the average person. Therefore, when confronted with such conditions, it becomes crucial for empaths to pause, reflect on their emotional state, and prioritize actions to restore emotional equilibrium and overall well-being, rather than persisting through the challenges.

17

How Empathy Works

Understanding Empathy

Despite our limited understanding of how empathy works, some information sheds light on its mechanisms. Everything emits a vibrant frequency or vibration, perceptible to empaths who can discern even the most subtle changes beyond the scope of ordinary senses. Expressive words carry a lively pattern originating from the speaker, possessing a distinct significance to them. Behind each expression lies energy, also known as a forcefield.

For instance, emotions like hate generate intense impressions that swiftly convey the underlying sentiment. The word "hatred" becomes fortified, strengthened by the tone of voice. Empaths absorb these emotions, whether expressed verbally, thought internally, or transmitted without a physical or verbal manifestation.

Empaths, akin to poets in action, are inherently creative individuals—innate writers, singers, and musicians. Their diverse and continuous interests make them multifaceted contributors to the creative realm. Found across all walks of life and cultures worldwide, empaths can be identified in families, communities, workplaces, and broader societies. There isn't a singular defining characteristic, gender, profession, or label attributed to empaths; they exist everywhere and can be anyone.

Empaths serve as life's attentive listeners, frequently taking on roles as problem solvers, leaders, and avid learners. Where there's a problem, empaths believe a solution exists and persistently seek resolutions for their own satisfaction.

Empathic Perception and Understanding Others

Empaths possess the unique ability to perceive others on multiple levels, understanding not only spoken words but also the emotions and thoughts beneath the surface. Proficient in reading body language and eye movements, empaths excel in listening and advising. Often putting others' needs before their own, empaths are prevalent in compassionate professions such as healing, counseling, clergy, and healthcare.

While empaths tend to be reserved and withdrawn, favoring listening over speaking, they may include loners, individuals experiencing sadness or distress, dreamers, or even narcissists.

Empaths' Connection with Nature

Empaths harbor a profound passion for nature and appreciate its magnificent beauty. Often found immersed in the outdoors, whether strolling on a sunny beach or exploring tranquil forests, empaths use nature as a therapeutic release. Connecting with nature becomes essential for empaths to rejuvenate their senses and find peace amid their busy lives.

Some empaths gravitate towards specific aspects of nature, like bodies of water, while others feel a stronger connection to mountains or hills. Animals hold a special place in empaths' hearts, driven not by a desire for power but by a genuine love for these creatures. It's not uncommon for empaths to have multiple pets, dispelling stereotypes like "the crazy cat lady" and highlighting the empathic bond with animals.

Empaths exhibit a duality, manifesting both expressive and reclusive tendencies. They often remain silent when receiving compliments, taking time to process the praise. Rather than highlighting their own positive attributes, empaths are more inclined to articulate favorable qualities about others. In the realm of emotional connection, empaths can be highly expressive, openly discussing their feelings. However, they may also adopt an opposite stance, becoming reclusive and unresponsive as a defense mechanism to shield themselves from overwhelming experiences.

In their social interactions, empaths tend to focus on external dynamics, sometimes neglecting their own needs. Their empathic nature leans towards non-violence and peacemaking, seeking to restore harmony in situations of discord. Even when confronted, empaths aim to swiftly resolve or avoid conflicts, preferring peaceful resolutions. They may harbor resentment if compelled to defend themselves with harsh words, striving to address issues with diplomacy.

Empaths find themselves deeply affected by various forms of media, such as TV, images, videos, and news broadcasts. They can be overwhelmed by depictions of violence or emotional dramas, often experiencing tears of empathy. Understanding cruelty becomes a challenging task for some empaths, as they grapple with the ignorance, closed-mindedness, and lack of compassion displayed by others.

The compassionate energy of empaths attracts individuals from diverse backgrounds and even animals. Strangers often find it easy to open up to empaths, sharing personal thoughts and feelings unintentionally. There is a subconscious recognition that empaths possess an innate understanding and empathy.

However, the negative side of empathy comes to the forefront as empaths are deeply sensitive to the emotions and energy of others. Their ability to absorb others' feelings can be challenging, especially when weak boundaries lead to taking on the pain and stress of those around them. Empaths, with their intuitive nature and deep insight, often become natural healers, navigating beyond surface-level experiences to understand individuals and situations at a profound level.

Individuals who possess empathic and highly sensitive traits can be likened to emotional detectives. Upon entering a room, they not only perceive the overall energy but also keenly tune into subtle shifts in facial expressions, changes in language, and discrepancies between verbal and non-verbal communication. The challenge lies in the fact that, often during their childhood, they were told they were too sensitive and even gaslighted, leading them to learn how to suppress these abilities to conform socially.

It's crucial to acknowledge that many highly sensitive individuals had to navigate challenging environments as children, essentially living in a warzone. To survive, they became adept at discerning minute signals and adapting to the slightest changes in their surroundings. This involved learning to anticipate the onset of a parent's rage or predicting when bullying might occur in the schoolyard.

While such experiences may foster hypervigilance, they also cultivate a heightened intuition about one's surroundings. Empaths find that their instincts are more often correct than incorrect, and what may be dismissed as "paranoia" often turns out to be an accurate reflection of aspects overlooked by others relying on surface-level interactions.

Their unparalleled ability to pick up on others' emotions in a nuanced manner is extraordinary. Empaths can sense the vibrant and high energy of a room, experiencing it as psychologically orgasmic. Conversely, when emotional vampires with envy and spite are present, empaths feel the "shock" of their draining influence. They can even detect subtle energies that others might miss, such as the undercurrent of jealousy in someone's heart.

Empaths can detect lies, even when individuals are deceiving themselves. They sense when something is "off" before noticeable shifts or strange sensations occur. Past trauma experiences, far from hindering their insights, actually enhance the accuracy of their readings. Some empaths may even directly feel another person's emotions, although they might not immediately comprehend them.

Empaths possess the ability to discern contempt beneath someone's niceties and detect hidden motives. Simultaneously, they can fully experience the authenticity of a person's soul when it shines through. Despite their unconventional insights, empaths often choose to remain silent and compliant, navigating internal turmoil while learning to listen.

Empowered empaths confidently utilize their skills without requiring external validation. They pursue their instincts and often achieve success, leaving those around them wondering about their unconventional methods. Their intuitive abilities, however, come at a cost: the need to develop unwavering self-belief despite external opinions.

Empathically empowered individuals understand the worth of this risk, as avoiding it would mean sacrificing their true selves and what they deeply know to be true. Toxic relationships, particularly with malignant narcissists, are attracted to empaths, as they recognize the wealth of energy, resources, and emotional support available. Narcissists seek to exploit empaths by attempting to control and accumulate their empathic resources to further their own agenda.

In conclusion, while toxic individuals may attempt to exploit empathy as a shortcut to their goals and reinforce their own needs, empathically empowered individuals are aware of the risks and consider them worthwhile to maintain their authenticity and deep understanding of truth.

18

Different Empathy Levels

Are you familiar with the three types of empathy and how to effectively convey them? Empathy is a crucial skill that adds simplicity to your life and relationships. Whether a student confides in you about feeling overwhelmed or your partner shares distressing news from work, your response matters. How would you react if your partner came home overwhelmed by fear, sadness, and anger due to job loss? The ideal response is one that is intelligent and compassionate.

It's essential to recognize that not all empathy looks the same, just as not all emotions, such as sadness, happiness, or fear, are identical. This is a topic that deeply concerns us at Heartmanity, especially since empathy plays a vital role in emotional intelligence (EQ) and connecting with loved ones and peers.

Consider the satisfaction of finishing work on a Friday compared to the joy of a wedding or the twisted pleasure of Schadenfreude (German for deriving joy from another's misfortune). Researchers have identified three types of empathy: Cognitive, Emotional, and Compassionate.

It's noteworthy that empathy is a relatively recent concept, still being defined by social and cognitive psychologists. "The term has only been around for about a century, but its significance has continually evolved." If empathy remains a vague concept for you, you can explore our article, "What is Empathy and Why is it Significant?"

Empathy is undeniably important, and the type of empathy you express or experience holds significance. Cognitive, Emotional, and Compassionate empathy manifest in various ways. Reflecting on your experiences at home, work, or with loved ones, you'll likely notice these different types in your own life. There are also numerous examples in TV, politics, and popular culture to draw from.

Cognitive Empathy, as defined by renowned psychologist and author Daniel Goleman in his book Emotional Intelligence (1995), involves understanding and knowing how another person feels and thinks. It encompasses perspective-taking and is primarily concerned with thought, understanding, and intellect. The benefits of Cognitive Empathy include facilitating communication, inspiring others, and gaining insight into diverse perspectives. However, it has its drawbacks, as it may detach from deep emotions and lack a felt sense of another's viewpoint.

Cognitive Empathy is characterized by intellectual comprehension rather than an emotional connection. Goleman illustrates this concept with an example of a partner's potential reaction to a surprising event, drawing parallels to a doctor analyzing a patient's illness without delving into their emotions. This form of empathy relies on mental capacity to respond to a situation. While it proves valuable in situations requiring understanding and consideration, it may be perceived as cold or disconnected, as it doesn't involve experiencing the emotions firsthand.

On the other hand, Emotional Empathy, as described by Goleman, involves genuinely sharing the emotions of another person as if they were contagious. This type of empathy is concerned with emotions, physical sensations, and the activation of mirror neurons in the brain. Emotional Empathy is beneficial in close interpersonal relationships and various professions like coaching, marketing, management, and human resources. However, it can be overwhelming or inappropriate in certain situations.

Unlike Cognitive Empathy, Emotional Empathy entails directly experiencing the emotions of others. It aligns with the concept of an "empath," someone capable of fully adopting another's emotional and mental state. This response may seem disconnected from rational thinking, but Goleman explains that emotional empathy is rooted in the mirror neurons of the human brain, similar to other animals. Emotional Empathy reacts to a situation by mirroring the emotions of the person involved.

When a loved one expresses intense emotions, Emotional Empathy triggers a natural response, pulling at the heartstrings and creating a deep, visceral reaction. However, like Cognitive Empathy, Emotional Empathy has its downsides. Goleman points out that individuals who struggle to manage their overwhelming emotions may experience psychological exhaustion leading to burnout. Excessive emotional empathy can make even minor interactions overwhelming.

Empathic Compassion

Defined as: "With this form of empathy, we not only grasp an individual's predicament and resonate with their feelings but are spontaneously inclined to assist, if necessary." - Daniel Goldman
What it involves: Intellect, emotion, and response.
Benefits: Considers the whole person.
Drawbacks: Few - this is the type of compassion we typically strive for!
In most cases, Empathic Compassion is ideal. Intellectual Empathy may be suitable for political or financial dealings or professional settings; Emotional Empathy may be the initial response for our loved ones; Empathic Compassion strikes a balance between the two.
Feelings of the heart and thoughts of the mind are not mutually exclusive. They are intricately connected. Empathic Compassion acknowledges this

natural connection by taking into account both the sensed emotions and intellectual context of another person.

When your loved one comes to you in tears, you want to understand why she is upset, and you also want to provide comfort by empathizing with her situation and hopefully assisting in her healing. It's a lot to handle!

Most of us will lean to one side or the other: either overly analytical or overly emotional. Empathic Compassion takes the middle ground and utilizes your emotional intelligence to respond to the situation appropriately. Should your partner simply be held? Does the situation call for swift action? Without becoming overwhelmed by sorrow or attempting to fix things with precision, empathy brings a delicate touch to the predicament.

When I think of compassion, I often envision a seesaw. Go too far into someone else's mind, and do you risk losing yourself? Avoid delving into their world, and are you missing out on a crucial part of the human experience? Is too much emotion inappropriate? Too little, detrimental?

Truly, most situations require a balance.

Can you recall one instance of each type of empathy in your own life? Likely more than one. Hopefully, you've encountered empathic compassion at one time or another!

Any example takes emotional well-being and practice - just like any other skill. When you find that sweet spot where you can relate, whether navigating a workplace hurdle or consoling a loved one, it is worth the effort.

Understanding Empathy and Empaths from a Scientific Perspective

Empathy represents the ability to step outside our self-centered viewpoints and perceive a situation from another person's standpoint. However, being an empath entails a deeper connection. Empaths, individuals positioned high on the empathic spectrum, experience and resonate with the emotions within their own bodies. This heightened empathy towards others can be profound, yet it often leaves empaths drained unless they establish strategies to safeguard their sensitivities and set firm boundaries.

1. The Role of Mirror Neuron System

Researchers have identified a specific cluster of brain cells responsible for fostering empathy, known as the mirror neuron system. These cells enable individuals to mirror emotions, empathizing with the pain, fear, or joy experienced by others. Empaths, believed to possess hyper-responsive mirror neurons, deeply resonate with the emotions of those around them. This phenomenon occurs as external events activate these mirror neurons, causing individuals to share the emotional experiences of others. Conversely, individuals with empathy deficiencies, such as psychopaths and narcissists, may exhibit an underactive mirror neuron system, rendering them incapable of experiencing unconditional love.

2. Electromagnetic Fields and Sensitivity

The next insight focuses on the electromagnetic fields generated by both the brain and the heart. According to the Heart Math Institute, these fields transmit information about people's thoughts and emotions. Empaths may exhibit heightened sensitivity to this electromagnetic input, becoming overwhelmed by it. Additionally, empaths often experience intensified physical and emotional responses to changes in the earth and sun's electromagnetic fields, understanding the impact of these changes on their mood and energy levels.

3. Emotional Contagion

Another key revelation contributing to our comprehension of empaths is the phenomenon of emotional contagion. Research indicates that many individuals unconsciously pick up on the emotions of those around them, leading to collective emotional experiences. Empaths, therefore, need to surround themselves with positive individuals to avoid being weighed down by negativity. Alternatively, if a friend is going through a challenging time, empaths should take precautions to ground themselves and maintain focus.

4. Dopamine Sensitivity Variation

The fourth discovery involves dopamine, a neurotransmitter linked to neuronal activity and the pleasure response. Studies reveal that introverted empaths tend to have higher dopamine sensitivity compared to extroverts. This heightened sensitivity means they require less dopamine to experience happiness. Consequently, introverted empaths find contentment in solitude, reading, and introspection, needing less external stimulation from social gatherings. In contrast, extroverts seek the dopamine surge from lively events, craving the excitement and energy associated with large social gatherings.

5. Synesthesia and Mirror-Touch Synesthesia

The fifth and intriguing finding introduces "mirror-touch synesthesia," a unique neurological condition that combines two distinct senses. In this case, individuals may feel the emotions and sensations of others in their bodies as if they were their own. This neurological explanation provides insight into the empathetic experience. As the Dalai Lama emphasizes, "Empathy is the human quality of greatest value," especially during challenging times when it's easy to feel overwhelmed.

19

Which Areas of the Empathic Lives?

B eing an empath has a pervasive impact on every aspect of your life. It differs from a regular job with set working hours; instead, the empathic experience is a constant, 24/7 occurrence. Consequently, no facet of your life remains untouched by your empathic abilities. While it's impossible to entirely shield your life from the influence of empathy, you can actively manage these effects, gaining control over your emotional environment's impact. This section will explore six distinct areas directly influenced by empathic abilities, shedding light on the challenges faced and proposing strategies for overcoming them.

Health

Empathic abilities commonly affect a person's health, with the continuous influx of emotions having both overwhelming and potentially devastating effects. Although complete avoidance of these effects is impossible when recognized, individuals can make decisions and choices that better safeguard their well-being. Physical symptoms, such as headaches, fatigue, and minor panic attacks, are often experienced due to prolonged exposure to large crowds, noisy environments, or harsh sensory inputs. These symptoms usually dissipate when empaths find a quiet space to rebalance their energies. However, if these symptoms persist, they may escalate into more severe forms like migraines, dizziness, nausea, and muscle pain. Empaths need to find solitude to undo the harmful effects of their environment, and daily meditation can enhance their resilience in emotionally charged settings.

In addition to affecting physical health, empathic abilities significantly influence emotional well-being. Lesser symptoms, like a general sense of sadness, low energy levels, and mild stress, can result from negative environments or interactions with people emitting negative emotions. Emotional exhaustion from helping others in need can also contribute to these symptoms. If unaddressed, these symptoms may escalate into more serious issues like depression, extreme anxiety, or even rage. It is crucial to seek solitude when experiencing such symptoms, as only then can one begin to counteract the detrimental effects of the environment. Regular meditation can also boost endurance in emotionally charged situations.

Addictions

Many empaths struggle with the constant flow of emotional energy that bombards their senses. While most find healthy coping mechanisms, some resort to less healthy methods, developing addictions to dull their senses and bring tranquility to their minds. Various addictions, including unhealthy eating habits, drinking alcohol, smoking, and compulsive shopping, serve as a means for empaths to self-medicate during bouts of depression and anxiety. Recognizing and addressing addictive behaviors is crucial to preventing long-term, harmful consequences. Seeking support from others or replacing unhealthy habits with activities like meditation and exercise can foster a shift towards healthier alternatives.

Emotional Bonds, Affection, and Intimacy

Regrettably, individuals with empathic tendencies often find themselves entangled in harmful relationships from which they struggle to break free. This phenomenon has two primary explanations. Initially, empaths are naturally drawn to those in need, driven by an inherent desire to provide support whenever possible. While this inclination may appear altruistic, it can inadvertently attract individuals with violent or self-destructive tendencies. Secondly, empathy compels individuals to stay connected with those requiring assistance. Consequently, even when recognizing the toxicity of a relationship, empaths feel trapped, unable to terminate it due to their aversion to causing suffering. Seeking counsel from friends or professionals proves instrumental in resolving this predicament.

Another challenge for empaths in relationships is their frequent emotional exhaustion, leaving them with insufficient energy to nurture a loving connection. Despite their yearning for deep relationships, empaths often prioritize others' happiness over their own. The remedy lies in finding a partner who possesses both vigor and understanding towards the empath's unique struggles.

Love and sexuality are profoundly influenced by empathic capabilities. While many perceive sex as an expression of love, empaths may view it as a means to ground themselves, dulling their heightened senses. This perspective can strain relationships, where one partner may feel more desired than genuinely loved during intimate moments. Emphatically, empaths engage in intimate encounters solely out of deep love, emphasizing the importance of consistently demonstrating affection.

Parenting

Navigating parenthood as an empath introduces unique challenges. Every empath was once a sensitive child, and many go on to start families, bringing empathic abilities into the realm of parenting. The heightened emotional connection between empathic parents and their children becomes both a blessing and a potential curse. Awareness of these challenges is crucial for effectively managing the impact of empathic abilities on family dynamics.

Parenting as an empath involves grappling with the overwhelming emotional input from children, especially considering the conflicting and confusing emotions typical in childhood. Detaching from this emotional whirlwind becomes essential to avoid being emotionally overwhelmed. Practices such as daily yoga or meditation prove beneficial. While sensing a child's suffering is an empathic advantage, it must not transform into an invasive tool, but rather used judiciously. Respecting a child's privacy, even when they refuse assistance, becomes paramount.

Children with empathic abilities may find life more challenging due to amplified guilt and sorrow for causing their parents distress. Emotional detachment is recommended to alleviate these effects.

Work

The workplace can significantly impact empaths, particularly in competitive environments. Empaths not only absorb their stress and anxiety but also that of those around them, making them exceptionally prone to stress. Establishing boundaries within the workplace is crucial for maintaining emotional balance and preventing burnout. Allocating alone time to recharge is vital, given the draining nature of the heightened emotional atmosphere at work. Ideally, empaths should seek autonomous roles to strike a balance between solitude and overwhelming stress.

Extraordinary Perceptual Abilities

This section has primarily addressed the challenges of empathic abilities, but there are positive aspects to embrace. As an empath, you may possess almost otherworldly abilities, such as glimpses into the future or distant events. Instead of fearing these gifts, embracing and developing them can lead to significant enhancements in various aspects of your life.

20

Are Empaths Born or Developed?

Similar to various human abilities, numerous researchers are intrigued by determining whether empathy is inherent or acquired. The recent upswing in interest in empathy has led to the emergence of several theories regarding its true origins and nature. Although no single theory fully elucidates this phenomenon, here are five of the most persuasive scientific theories from neuroscience experts.

Theory #1: Mirror Neurons

Researchers have pinpointed a specialized group of brain cells associated with compassion, termed "mirror neurons." These neurons enable individuals to mirror the emotions of others, suggesting that empaths possess hypersensitive mirror neurons, allowing them to feel others' joy, sadness, fear, and pain. Advocates of this theory propose that empaths are born with these mirror neurons, present from birth, explaining why some babies seem to empathize.

Theory #2: Electromagnetic Fields

Rooted in the discovery that both the brain and heart generate electromagnetic fields, this theory suggests these fields serve as conduits for the transmission of thoughts and emotions between individuals. Highly empathetic people are thought to be more receptive to these signals, suggesting a sensitivity present from birth. However, this theory does not rule out the possibility of developing sensitivity over time with proper techniques.

Theory #3: Emotional Contagions

According to this theory, emotions, like diseases, can be picked up by individuals through proximity to those experiencing them. While not focused on the origins of empathy, this theory implies a natural ability to pick up emotional contagions, suggesting a predisposition from birth. It does not, however, dismiss the notion that empathy can be learned and improved.

Theory #4: Increased Dopamine Sensitivity

Some neuroscientists posit that empaths, particularly introverts, are more sensitive to dopamine, a neurotransmitter associated with pleasure. Introverted empaths supposedly have lower pleasure thresholds, requiring less dopamine than extraverts to feel happy. This theory aligns with the idea that empathy, like introversion and extraversion, is present at birth, influenced by both genetics and environmental factors.

Theory #5: Mirror-Touch Synesthesia

Drawing parallels with mirror-touch synesthesia, a rare neurological condition where individuals process sensory stimuli in multiple ways, this theory suggests empathy is akin to this condition. Synesthetic individuals with mirror-touch could feel others' emotions and physical sensations as if they were their own. While not providing strong arguments for being born as an empath, this theory acknowledges synesthesia can occur either at birth or due to a specific trauma.

In comparison to these neuroscientific theories, human development experts propose that empathy is a learned ability. According to their case studies, parental support during childhood is the main contributing factor, with genetics serving as an indicator rather than a definitive determinant. The type of upbringing an individual receives plays a crucial role in determining their level of empathy, even if predisposed due to parental empathic abilities.

- Parenting characterized by abuse or neglect

Research on the early stages of child development indicates that traumas experienced during this period can have a profound impact on an individual's emotional sensitivity and response to various stimuli in adulthood. Many individuals seeking professional assistance for empathic traits often originate from households where one or both parents struggle with depression, alcoholism, or violence.

The absence of care and support erodes a person's natural defenses, leading to the heightened vulnerability of empaths to negative emotions from their surroundings. Additionally, lacking effective emotional management skills, empaths in this category are more prone to absorbing and being unable to distinguish external energies and emotions from their own.

- Nurturing Parenting

Research emphasizes the influential role parents play as early role models, particularly for children displaying empathic characteristics. Consequently, the words and actions of parents significantly contribute to the healthy development of these children's unique gifts.

Lessons acquired in early childhood continue to evolve throughout one's life. Depending on the level of support from parents, these learned behaviors may either intensify or diminish. Empaths raised in nurturing environments tend to develop superior coping mechanisms compared to those in less favorable conditions. Their enhanced ability to navigate the challenges of being an empath enables them to utilize their gifts in meaningful and beneficial ways for themselves and those around them.

While the origins of empathic traits remain unclear, efforts to unravel this mystery are not in vain. Each piece of information gained proves valuable for empaths seeking guidance on maintaining health and functionality in the complexities of the modern world.

21

Emotional Intelligence and Empathy

On Monday morning, Steve entered his office and discovered his secretary, Pamela, slouched in her chair, staring blankly at her desk with a noticeable frown and a downturned mouth that reflected sadness. Unresponsive to Steve's morning greeting, Pamela remained motionless. Steve placed his bag on his desk and approached Pamela, gently touching her shoulders. Startled, she snapped back to the present, quickly putting on a forced smile, and greeted Steve.

Concerned, Steve inquired about her well-being. Despite brushing away tears, Pamela insisted she was fine and returned to her tasks. However, Steve persisted, inviting her to his office and encouraging her to share her concerns. Demonstrating not only concern for his staff but also organizational intelligence, Steve recognized that addressing Pamela's emotional state was crucial for her optimal performance.

Steve's approach showcased emotional intelligence and nonviolent communication skills, aiming to build trust and empathy. This strategy not only addressed Pamela's immediate problem but also had long-term implications for the company's productivity by fostering a positive work environment with content and supported employees.

The example illustrates the effectiveness of demonstrating empathy, a crucial element in effective communication. Empathy enhances social interaction, sharpens social awareness, and enables quick and effective responses to nonverbal cues. In the stress-filled modern era, empathy is often lacking, as the culture prioritizes winning, success, and competition.

Defined as the ability to recognize, identify, understand, and be sensitive to another person's thoughts and emotions without sharing the same experiences, empathy is essential due to our biological need for attachment, connection, belonging, and validation. Unfortunately, contemporary culture often neglects empathy in the pursuit of individual success, contributing to a lack of understanding and respect for diverse experiences.

Empathy, adopted into the English language a century ago from the German word "Einfühlung," meaning "feeling into," is a critical aspect of communication. It involves fully hearing, understanding, and respecting another person's experience without necessarily agreeing with their ideas. Providing empathy doesn't imply endorsing someone's perspective but acknowledges and respects their feelings and thoughts. Reflecting and paraphrasing what was heard signals active engagement in the conversation, demonstrating a full presence and understanding of the speaker.

After the speaker feels heard and understood, they may seek your opinion. Presenting your viewpoints objectively, supported by reasons, is appropriate at this stage. Thus, showing empathy doesn't compel agreement but fulfills the need for the speaker to be fully heard and understood.

Empathy versus Sympathy

Empathy is characterized as the capacity to recognize, acknowledge, and understand the emotions of another person by viewing situations from their perspective. When practicing empathy, one shares in the sadness or distress of another without personally undergoing the same experience. In contrast, sympathy involves a sense of 'community feeling' or 'fellow feeling,' lacking the emotional sharing found in empathy. For instance, if someone reveals they are feeling depressed after losing their mother, responding with, 'I lost my mother last year, and I know exactly what you are going through,' demonstrates sympathy rather than empathy. Empathy entails hearing and comprehending the other person's viewpoint without directly experiencing the same emotions or situations.

Empathy and Emotional Intelligence

Empathy serves as the cornerstone of emotional intelligence and nonviolent communication. When encouraging someone to empathize with another, the directive is often, 'Put yourself in their shoes.' Empathy facilitates communication by grasping the ideas, thoughts, and emotions of others.

The Significance of Empathy in Emotional Intelligence

Enhanced empathy fosters a deeper connection with our humanity, resulting in more meaningful and robust relationships. In professional settings, empathy contributes to success, promoting a healthier and happier life overall. Success in various forms, especially those involving teamwork, relies on the heightened emotional intelligence of leaders and team members. The cultivation of emotional intelligence typically initiates with the leader, and team members acquire these skills through learning.

Empathy Builds Lasting Relationships

Empathy establishes sustained relationships by fostering trust, openness, and an improved understanding of others' thoughts and ideas. Building trust and openness occurs as individuals recognize your empathy, leading them to confide in you. Trust increases over time, allowing for the sharing of more information, thoughts, and feelings.

For example, if you notice a team member appears troubled, expressing concern by saying, 'I can see that something is bothering you. Would you like to talk about it?' demonstrates empathy. An emotionally intelligent response acknowledges their hesitation and reassures them of your friendship and willingness to help whenever they are ready to talk.

Improving Understanding Through Empathy

Empathy involves focused listening, where distractions are set aside to comprehend both spoken and unspoken aspects of communication. While empathy cannot read minds, it enables a deep understanding of what someone is going through by paying attention to verbal and nonverbal cues.

Empathy and Nonverbal Communication

Demonstrating empathy and emotional intelligence extends to both verbal and nonverbal communication. Strategies for enhancing empathy through nonverbal communication include active and engaged listening, sitting next to the person, mirroring body language, and maintaining a relaxed facial expression.

Avoiding Pitfalls in Expressing Empathy

Despite understanding the power of empathy, common pitfalls can inadvertently make individuals feel worse. Comparing their situation to a seemingly worse one or insisting on looking at the positive side may invalidate their feelings. Genuine empathy involves avoiding comparisons and allowing individuals to express their emotions without imposing a positive perspective.

22

Different Ways to Overcome Anxiety as An Empath

A nxiety has become a prevalent issue not just for individuals with empathic abilities but for the general population as well. The drawback of being an empath is the heightened susceptibility to anxiety, surpassing that of others, leading to a profound sense of exhaustion. The innate capacity of empaths to easily absorb the emotions of others contributes significantly to their frequent struggles with anxiety, often making them more susceptible to depression. However, managing and mitigating anxiety issues is imperative for those aspiring to maintain a well-balanced and healthy life.

Certainly, verbal communication is not the sole indicator of an individual's disposition. Empaths possess the ability to sense the energy enveloping a person, providing valuable insights into their emotional state or experiences. Negative energy, when absorbed by empaths, can have adverse effects on their well-being. Furthermore, empaths have the knack for discerning unspoken thoughts and subtle nuances of meaning from others, and when they start behaving like emotional sponges, the world can become overwhelming.

During their teenage years, empaths often grapple with low self-esteem, and if not addressed promptly, matters can spiral out of control. Signs of anxiety manifest early in adolescence, setting the stage for a cycle of confusion, depression, and intense anxiety. As they transition into their 20s, the responsibilities they must juggle exacerbate the bouts of anxiety. Regardless of the stage of life one finds oneself in, encountering this book provides an opportunity to implement strategies that can effectively combat and overcome anxiety in day-to-day life.

Remember, You Aren't Accountable for Everything

If you find resonance with the sentiments expressed above, it's crucial to acknowledge that you are not responsible for the emotions of others. Likewise, others are not to blame for your own feelings. Always bear in mind that honesty entails courage, and vulnerability embodies strength. While you can attempt to influence someone's emotions, ultimately, it is within their control how they interpret a given situation. This realization may take time to settle in, but once it does, your perspective on life will undergo a profound transformation.

Empaths often grapple with a sense of responsibility for everything and strive relentlessly to mend situations, even without solicitation. Their inclination is to love and give more. However, this mindset is flawed. Liberation comes when you comprehend that the entire world's responsibility doesn't rest solely on your shoulders. Empaths, attuned to internalizing every emotion they encounter, must repeatedly remind themselves that there are limits to what one person can do for another. The rest is in the hands of the other individual.

Another common pitfall for empaths is being so focused on fixing others that they overlook whether the person is comfortable with their distress and has no desire to be rescued. Once the self-blame diminishes, a significant reduction in anxiety often follows.

Embrace Your Emotions, Don't Avoid Them

Growing up, you may have been advised not to cry over trivial matters, fostering a habit of avoiding situations that induce negative emotions. Contrary to this practice, it's essential to confront your emotions from childhood onward. The instinct to avoid should be replaced with a readiness to confront these emotions directly. While it might seem counterintuitive for an empath to advocate facing stuffed emotions, doing so releases pent-up energy in a healthy manner.

Accumulated energy leads to anxiety and panic attacks, a result of empaths suppressing and avoiding their feelings in their focus on others. Attempting to escape emotions only perpetuates a cycle of suffering and anxiety. Instead, consider your feelings akin to waves in an ocean—coming and going. Facing emotions not only helps you grow but imparts valuable life lessons.

Avoiding emotions is akin to applying a Band-Aid to a wound that requires proper care. It provides momentary relief but doesn't address the underlying issue. Negative coping strategies like avoidance exacerbate the situation. Develop a nonjudgmental stance, study your emotions, and build effective coping strategies.

Recognize When You're Projecting Emotions onto Others

Understanding the concept of projection is crucial for every empath. While empaths often act as emotional sponges, absorbing others' feelings, they also experience their own emotions deeply. Distinguishing personal feelings from others' is challenging, but it's a vital lesson for empaths.

Projection occurs when an empath attributes their unconscious impulses to others. For instance, if a friend faces adversity and grieves, an empath might empathize but unintentionally project their own imagined grief onto the friend. These projections complicate relationships and lead to unnecessary problems. To avoid this, refrain from assuming others' feelings—ask directly for clarity, preventing the creation of false narratives and promoting a better understanding of the truth.

Build Your Self-Confidence

Individuals who possess empathy but grapple with low self-esteem often undergo significant challenges. The constant influx of stimuli faced by empaths on a daily basis can easily disrupt their mental equilibrium, leading to confusion and a descent into feelings of worthlessness and hopelessness. This, in turn, triggers various forms of anxiety in empaths. The key to overcoming such a predicament lies in boosting one's self-esteem.

Stay Attuned to Your Body

Empaths are deeply impacted not only on a physical level but also on a profound emotional level by the feelings and emotions of others. In certain instances, as empaths absorb the emotions of those around them, they may become so saturated over time that symptoms such as headaches, pains, and fatigue become apparent. These symptoms intensify, particularly when the empath is grappling with anxiety. To effectively address anxiety, it is essential to be mindful of your body and pay attention to these symptoms.

A common question for empaths is, 'where do I begin?' Starting with grounding techniques can be beneficial in managing heightened emotions, which are often the root causes of anxiety. Engaging in yoga is a popular choice, and establishing a routine with simple asanas aids the body in the destressing process. Spending time in nature, such as taking walks in parks, has proven calming effects on the senses.

If time constraints hinder these activities, consider getting a massage, particularly Ayurvedic massages known for relieving stress and negative energies from the body. To promote overall well-being, it's crucial to be attuned to the signals your body is displaying.

Abandon the Shielding Technique

The shielding technique, wherein empaths attempt to shield themselves from negative energies, proves ineffective in the long run. While it may offer momentary relief, it is only temporary. The primary drawback of this technique lies in its language of victimhood. Identifying as a victim hinders true healing; resisting negative energy sets one on a cycle of pain and fear without achieving lasting healing.

The solution involves transforming the shield into a filter—a permeable barrier that repels negative energies while allowing positive energies to pass through. Constant shielding prevents the experience of many positive aspects of life. Understanding that feeling others' emotions to a certain extent is harmless is crucial. The challenge arises when absorbing unhealthy emotions triggers anxiety and depression.

Alternatively, drop the shield but learn to detach from malevolent energies. Empaths tend to adopt any amount of negative energy and make it their own, an unnecessary level of surrogacy. It's essential to practice a healthy level of detachment from inconsequential matters that could adversely affect mental health. Achieving this detachment requires a degree of rationality to discern which issues warrant attention and which do not. In simpler terms, adopting a non-emotional perspective when faced with life's crossroads is key.

23

Change Your Mindset

I hold the belief that success and happiness are intricately tied to our mindsets, influencing every aspect of our lives, including our reactions and responses to the world around us. Aligning your mindset with your aspirations is crucial for achieving your goals.

The journey towards self-improvement starts with recognizing the impact of your self-talk on your mindset. Transforming negative self-talk into empowering affirmations can significantly shape your perspective. Embrace self-encouragement, recognizing that your own words hold the most significant influence.

Moreover, your mindset reflects how you perceive yourself. Constantly reinforcing negative beliefs about yourself, such as being untidy or an inadequate worker, ingrains these thoughts in your mind. Engaging in positive literature can swiftly shift your thinking, with careful selection based on genres and titles. Opt for motivating and uplifting books, journaling to track the evolution of your mindset.

Utilizing your surroundings to shape your thinking is particularly effective for individuals with empathic tendencies. Acknowledging the vastness of the world beyond oneself can break the shackles of a limiting mindset. Nature serves as a rejuvenating escape, cleansing the mind and fostering appreciation for life's beauty. Sunshine, as a natural mood-booster, enhances the clarity needed for continued self-improvement.

Surrounding yourself with like-minded individuals and celebrating daily achievements contribute to your overall success. Remember, everyone experiences moments of self-doubt, influenced by external opinions and internal thoughts. Taking charge of your feelings and thoughts is essential; resist letting others dictate your self-worth.

An inner critic, fueled by external opinions and internal doubts, can hinder self-esteem. Counter this by shutting down the inner critic and redirecting your focus. Create a list of confidence-boosting elements for challenging days, preserving positive messages in visible places like the bathroom mirror.

Comparisons to others are inevitable, but acknowledging that there will always be someone seemingly "better" is crucial. Embrace your uniqueness; being yourself is more important than outperforming others. Social media often fosters unrealistic ideals, leading to feelings of inadequacy. Reject the notion of perfection and engage in activities that bring joy and positivity, promoting kindness towards oneself.

Procrastination, a common obstacle, can impede progress. To effect change, take responsibility for your decisions and actions. Resist the allure of reasons not to change, and instead, make deliberate choices aligned with your desired direction. Even small steps contribute to progress, so document your journey and remain patient throughout the transformation process.

Embarking on self-improvement demands dedication, recognizing that positive changes take time. Choose one significant change, commit to it, and celebrate the incremental progress. You are worth the effort, and as you persevere, you'll discover the value in taking those initial steps toward a more fulfilling life.

Explore Your Empathic Nature with These Inquiries

The provided questions aim to dispel any uncertainties surrounding your identity as an empath.

1. Do you feel overwhelmed when entering crowded places like markets? Unlike most individuals who find joy in market visits, empaths may experience fear due to their heightened sensitivity to absorbing others' energies, particularly negative ones.

2. Can you instantly perceive personal details about people that they haven't shared with you? Some empaths possess intuitive abilities that reveal hidden stories about individuals upon meeting them, appearing almost like a dream but rooted in their sharp intuition.

3. Do you become unwell immediately after meeting someone? Empaths, being highly sensitive, can often sense when someone harbors harmful intentions towards others.

4. Did you witness unusual phenomena during childhood, such as ghosts, alien sightings, or interactions with imaginary friends? Many empaths report mysterious childhood experiences that they rarely disclose to others.

5. Can you sense the energy emitted by buildings? Empaths can discern whether a building carries positive or negative energy and may even gauge the energies of its recent inhabitants.

6. Are you labeled as antisocial? Empaths may prefer small, tight-knit friend groups over large social gatherings to avoid being drained by the diverse energies encountered in larger groups.

7. Do you notice intricate details that others might overlook? Empaths tend to observe specific details, not just superficial qualities, about things or people,

showcasing an extraordinary level of perceptiveness.

8. Can you read people's minds or discern their true thoughts even when unspoken? Empaths often pick up on the unspoken thoughts and emotions of others, even when the person tries to hide their true feelings.

9. Do people easily open up to you? Despite typically minimizing interactions, empaths find that others are drawn to them, seeking support and viewing them as potential saviors.

10. Are you skilled at detecting lies? Empaths can often discern honesty or deceit with just a glance into someone's eyes, making them adept at identifying falsehoods, which can be a source of concern for them.

11. Do your friends complain about your sensitivity? Empaths have likely been sensitive since childhood, reacting strongly to negative stimuli like violent scenes on TV or the utterance of a wrong word.

12. Are you adept at spotting fake people? Empaths can sense when others are being disingenuous, perceiving the emotional and mental makeup of those who pretend to be something they are not.

13. Are you exceptionally compassionate? Empaths stand out for their boundless compassion, always willing to help those in need and yearning for others to embrace similar levels of empathy.

14. Do you experience others' feelings as if they were your own? This classic empathic quality involves feeling the emotions of others as intensely as if they were one's own, often leading to a sudden shift in emotional states when in the company of others.

24

How to Get Rid of Toxic and Negative Peopleand Negative Energy

The term "toxic individuals" refers to people who are likely to undermine and hinder your growth instead of supporting it. Negative individuals are those with a pessimistic outlook on life, focusing selectively on the negatives in any situation and disregarding the positive aspects. Negativity has the potential to spread from one person to another, impacting an individual's level of success. Negative individuals tend to harbor negative thoughts, and when surrounded by such harmful influences, one's ambitions may wither, leading to a loss of focus on achieving personal goals. Identifying and avoiding negative individuals requires awareness of specific qualities to watch out for.

Negative people are prone to negative thought processes, as suggested by cognitive theories. Our thinking patterns and the values we attribute to ourselves significantly influence our perspectives on the world, ourselves, and others. Pessimistic beliefs and thoughts can result in mental and emotional suffering, with a heightened risk of mood and anxiety disorders. Constant self-defeating beliefs are characteristic of negative individuals, encompassing their values, attitudes, and personal views, which can be either interpersonal or intrapersonal. Interpersonal beliefs impact self-perception, while interpersonal beliefs shape views of others, involving concepts such as fear of conflicts, submissiveness, and blame. Intrapersonal mindsets pertain to underachievement, approval, and perfectionism.

Negative thinking patterns, also known as cognitive distortions, are thoughts that arise in challenging situations. For instance, if one believes that tasks must be executed perfectly and receives negative feedback on a project, self-defeating thoughts may emerge, leading to feelings of inadequacy or comparisons with others. Life challenges trigger negative thoughts that can lead to overthinking and exaggeration, making it harder for individuals to overcome difficulties. Faced with such challenges, individuals may perceive themselves as failures and may attribute blame to internal or external factors. Persistent negative thoughts adversely affect self-worth and increase the risk of mental illnesses.

Destructive Relationships

Associating with toxic and pessimistic individuals is likely to contaminate your mindset with their cynical perspective on life. Their thoughts significantly shape a person's actions. Being in a relationship or friendship with a toxic individual can introduce chaos into various aspects of your life:

You find yourself constantly solving a barrage of problems created by the toxic person. Seeking attention, they involve others in addressing issues that arise frequently, some of which are of their own making as they strive to have people around caring for them.

Your comfort with your own life and progress towards your goals diminishes. Friendships with toxic individuals can derail your life by diverting you from your objectives. The person demands undivided attention, and if you're not careful, you may sideline your goals to meet their demands. The person's negativity can overwhelm your positivity, depleting you of your positive energy.

You feel drained after interacting with them. Dealing with toxic individuals is exhausting, both physically and emotionally. Listening to their complaints about trivial matters and their negative views on others and life, in general, can affect your mental well-being.

Their presence fills you with anxiety. If you can't distance yourself from a toxic family member or close friend, you reluctantly tolerate them, anticipating their behavior and attitude with a desire to get it over with.

You feel exhausted from their constant drama. Toxic individuals thrive on creating scenes to attract attention. If you're a non-toxic person, the experience is far from enjoyable. You avoid interacting with them, especially in public settings, to steer clear of their drama.

Being with them makes you feel disconnected from your true self. You either feel pushed around or respond by trying to control the toxic person. Their persistent demands may drive you to act excessively controlling to avoid being manipulated at their whim.

You become overly self-conscious and cautious. In the company of toxic people, you can't predict their behavior, which often goes against societal norms. Walking on eggshells becomes a regular feeling.

Managing Negative Thoughts

Personal beliefs are shaped by a person's lifetime experiences and the environment they grew up in. Altering these beliefs is challenging, as they form an integral part of one's being. Negative thought patterns are not easily identifiable.

To manage negative thoughts, start by consciously acknowledging them as they arise. During challenges, observe your thought patterns shifting from seeking solutions to self-defeating thoughts.

Identify these negative thoughts and challenge them by seeking evidence to support your conclusions. This involves introducing rational questioning, assessing the credibility and trustworthiness of the information source, and verifying the accuracy of supporting facts. Discard thoughts that lack sufficient substantiation.

Replace negative thoughts with positive ones. Embracing positivity and letting go of negativity trains the brain to focus on positive aspects. While challenging negative thoughts may initially seem difficult, consistent practice makes it a natural process. Adopting Socratic questioning aids in questioning the validity of conclusions, contributing to effective decision-making.

Efficient Management of Negative and Harmful Individuals

As previously discussed, the impact of having individuals with a negative and toxic influence in our lives is considerable. The stress, anxiety, and tension experienced when surrounded by such people can lead to the severing of connections. Successfully dealing with negative and toxic individuals requires a heightened level of self-awareness. It is crucial for a person to understand their strengths and weaknesses, identify what they can handle, recognize their limits, and apply intelligence in managing such relationships. The following are some guidelines on how to navigate interactions with negative and toxic individuals.

In handling toxic and negative people, it becomes necessary to establish boundaries. Negative individuals often seek to monopolize attention by focusing on their never-ending problems, aiming more for personal satisfaction than a healthy relationship. To avoid being drawn into unproductive conversations without appearing rude, refrain from indulging them. Redirect the discussion towards genuine concerns by prompting them to discuss potential solutions to their issues. Often, the individual may lack interest in addressing the problems they share, and when they realize you are not readily engaging in non-productive talk, they will likely avoid involving you.

During conflicts with toxic and negative individuals, they may generate drama to seek constant attention and raise arguments on baseless issues. It is important to choose battles wisely, selecting those where you can prevail without succumbing to emotional drainage or negativity. Remember, there is no trophy for the winner. Allow the dust to settle, and articulate your point when the opportune moment arises.

Avoid becoming emotionally entangled in the actions and behavior of toxic individuals. Apply logic instead of letting emotions take over. When faced with attempts to engage in competition, detach your feelings from the situation. By maintaining emotional composure and employing logical reasoning, you discourage the person from continuing their disruptive behavior.

Exercise caution with your emotions when interacting with toxic and cynical individuals. You are accountable for your actions, and your reactions to their behavior can either encourage or discourage their pursuit. Resist acting impulsively and allow the moment to pass, as a less emotionally charged time will present itself for effective action. Allowing emotions to escalate the drama can derail your focus.

Establish and adhere to boundaries based on your observations of the individual's thinking and behavior. Recognize times when the person is more likely to cause disruptions, and interact with them during periods of stability and in environments where they are less likely to act out. This approach preserves your relationships and prevents you from being engulfed in their drama.

Refuse to let others determine your emotions, as everyone seeks happiness. Shield yourself from absorbing the emotions of negative individuals by adhering to logic. Negative people may criticize and make derogatory remarks, but it is crucial not to let such comments disturb your pursuit of happiness. Know yourself, your strengths, and weaknesses; external opinions should not significantly affect you. Avoid spending excessive time validating or arguing points, as prolonged engagement with criticism can negatively impact your self-esteem.

It's essential to note that when individuals aim to affect you negatively, they may exaggerate their remarks. While you cannot control their thoughts and opinions, you can manage how their comments influence your life.

25

Finding Empathic Joy

When you eliminate negative energy from your life, it's important to replace the void left by negativity with sources of pure joy and positivity. While there might be an inclination to resort to vices or addictions during this time, opting for healthier practices can yield long-term benefits. Choosing activities such as nurturing plants, immersing yourself in nature, spending time with animals or children, and engaging in creative expressions over alcohol, adrenaline rushes, or sexual gratification can contribute to nurturing positivity within, avoiding energy depletion, and maintaining balance.

For instance, tending to plants and connecting with nature, even for those not inherently plant-empathetic, can help rejuvenate faith in one's abilities and the magic of the universe. Nature, in turn, aids in spiritual awakening, emotional balance, and purging emotional contagion. Spending time with animals or young children, especially for empaths, can provide a natural high, as these spirits resonate empathetically, bringing laughter, inhibitions release, and a reminder of unconditional love.

Creative expressions play a vital role in preventing an empath from becoming an emotional powder keg. Whether through one's life passion or exploring different artistic mediums, artistic expression helps channel messages and achieve a sense of catharsis. Depending on empath types, such as plant empaths or physical empaths, activities like acting or dancing may be particularly beneficial. Acting, similar to gardening, involves planting ideas and nurturing them to fruition. Dancing helps physical empaths stay grounded while expressing emotions.

For geomantic empaths, sculpting, woodwork, stone carving, or working with healing crystals and gemstones can be meditative and expressive. Animal empaths may find joy in singing or other musical forms, as it utilizes non-verbal elements akin to animal communication while articulating human concepts like rhythm and harmony. Emotional empaths, being the most common, resonate well with painting, illustration, poetry, and prose writing, allowing them to translate intangible emotions into precise, defined, and permanent mediums.

Joining a Collective with a Shared Objective

As empaths are attuned to various energy levels, they often experience a sense of ongoing conflict within their energy fields. The diverse goals pursued by individuals globally, whether significant or minor, frequently clash with one another, leading empaths to feel drained or, in severe cases, susceptible to depression and hopelessness.

To counteract these emotions, actively participating in a group that regularly collaborates towards a common goal can be highly beneficial. In a well-managed group with members who predominantly have sincere intentions, a harmonious atmosphere can contribute to revitalizing energy and restoring faith in humanity. Opting for activities such as joining a singing group or choir, affiliating with a church or faith-based organization, or engaging in collaborative projects devoid of internal competition, can be particularly effective. This creates a sense of empowerment, value, and connection to the world, contrasting with the feeling of being adrift or in conflict with it.

Caution should be exercised when considering groups solely focused on fundraising, as environments primarily centered around money may not align well with empathic sensitivities. While fundraising and earning money legitimately are commendable pursuits, empaths may find their energies better utilized elsewhere due to their natural inclination to avoid seizing power from others or accumulating more than necessary.

Physical Expression

Empaths often grapple with mental and emotional overload, balancing personal emotions while deflecting negative energies and welcoming positive and neutral ones. To remain focused, present, and grounded, frequent physical manifestation becomes crucial. This involves projecting one's intricate inner world into the physical realm through practices like daily gratitude lists, expressing desires or personal priorities, or engaging in creative forms of manifestation such as painting mental imagery, dancing, songwriting, or collage-making. Some empaths may prefer manifestation rituals involving crystal healing, celestial alignments, or prayer to divine entities. With experimentation and dedication, finding a manifestation ritual that energizes, balances, and stabilizes emotions becomes attainable, creating a mindset akin to a well-prepared kitchen counter that facilitates efficient and easy management of life's challenges.

Forgiveness

The concept of forgiveness holds substantial weight, as studies in psychology and neuroscience attest to its profound positive effects on both the forgiver and the forgiven. For empaths, who may have experienced deep hurts in past relationships, moving on, letting go of caring, or releasing angry sentiments can be challenging. Forgiveness, however, transcends notions of justice and fairness that empaths highly value. Instead, it is about liberating oneself from negative energy and creating space for joy. Rather than pondering whether the person deserves forgiveness, empaths are encouraged to ask themselves if they are ready to shed the burden of anger, pain, and hurt feelings, and if they are prepared to progress forward emotionally.

26

The Overall Experience of a Person's Empathic Healing

The widespread and widely acknowledged phenomenon concerning empathy is that it can be viewed as both a blessing and a curse. Experiencing empathy involves feeling things deeply, living through them entirely, and sensing every nuance. Empathy goes beyond merely sharing the experiences of others; it encompasses the ability to perceive and comprehend the unspoken and hidden aspects, including the subtle energies individuals carry with them. These energies, often referred to as vibes, vary in interpretation, with some viewing them skeptically, considering them not as vibes but as a person's inherent capacity to sense and reflect. Despite being poorly understood by many, empathy is an innate personality trait residing within an individual's instincts. It enables the observation of others' innermost thoughts and emotions, not only understanding them but also experiencing them as if they were one's own. Empaths are commonly recognized as silent observers of the world, attuned not only to humans but also to the natural world and its various inhabitants. They embody a deep connection to nature and its essence.

The Empath Healing Experience of an Individual

Empathy can be described both as a personality trait and, in a negative sense, as a affliction. In the latter context, the idea is that absorbing other people's emotions and resonating with their intense feelings can make an individual emotionally vulnerable and physically unwell. The inclination to focus excessively on others' problems and the pessimistic aspects of life can lead empaths to self-inflicted harm, where their emotional sensitivity takes a toll on their mental health. Empaths are akin to compassionate individuals who, in their selflessness, neglect their well-being to assist others, inadvertently causing harm to themselves. Labeling empathy as a disease may not be universally accepted, as it does not manifest as a clear and recognizable physical ailment within society. Nevertheless, the existence of empathy and the internal struggles faced by empaths, whether due to their uncontrollable actions or difficulty in understanding certain aspects, necessitate support in the modern world. The detailed document below delves into the empath healing experience, offering valuable insights to individuals of this nature, aiding them in navigating the challenges associated with this empathetic facet of life.

1. To recover from the internal wounds caused by empathy, the initial step for an empath involves recognizing that they are not accountable for the pain or emotional and physical decline of others. Being empathetic means understanding the dynamics of absorbing everyone's emotions and pain, living with these sensations, and desiring peace. At times, the empath may exert more effort than the person facing problems, leading to feelings of inadequacy when unable to bring about a satisfactory resolution. It's crucial for empaths to grasp their limitations, acknowledging that they can offer support within certain boundaries, but cannot single-handedly rectify every situation. Empaths must realize that caring deeply does not grant the power to force others into self-improvement if they are unwilling to make the necessary efforts.

2. A second essential lesson for empaths is that avoiding the pain they feel is not a solution. Running away from pain doesn't facilitate healing

or coping; instead, it exacerbates the struggle. It may seem counterintuitive to confront the pain one is attempting to escape, but it is the correct path to resolution. Understanding and acknowledging internal pain and emotional distress are the initial steps, followed by releasing these emotions. Much like a compressed spring, suppressing emotions without addressing them only intensifies the struggle. Empaths need to sit down, confront the emotions they are evading, experience the fatigue, reflect on the confusion, and recognize the built-up anger. This initial confrontation is crucial for understanding and ultimately overcoming confusion, hurt, and pain.

3. A crucial aspect of empath healing involves recognizing that not all experienced pain is necessarily someone else's. Despite the common assumption that empaths absorb others' pain, they need to pause and reflect on the origin of the pain they feel. Distinguishing between their own pain and that of others is vital for effective healing. Often, individuals projecting blame for feeling someone else's pain overlook the possibility that they themselves might be struggling. Detecting and discerning between personal pain and external influences is fundamental to navigating the empathetic healing process.

4. Another key consideration for empath healing is acknowledging that low self-esteem hinders the recovery process. Boosting self-esteem is essential for overcoming internal struggles. A direct correlation exists between an empath's high self-esteem and the efficacy of the healing process. Feelings of worthlessness and unlovability, common among empaths, combined with an inability to solve others' problems, contribute to self-hate and underestimation. Building self-love, respect, trust, hope, care, and affection progressively aids in healing empathic wounds, counteracting negative thoughts about one's worth and importance.

5. A clear distinction exists between having empathy and being an empath. While empathy entails feeling sorry for others and offering support, being an empath goes beyond, involving a deeper understanding of others' emotions,

actions, and energies. Recognizing this difference is crucial for both empaths and those around them, as empaths do not equate to empathy, and their struggles require distinct approaches.

6. Empaths are often advised to shield themselves from surrounding energies. Shielding involves creating a protective barrier by focusing on tasks or oneself to appear unaffected by external influences. However, shielding is not a definitive solution; it may temporarily keep energies at bay but leads to internal struggles and repressed emotions. Empaths seeking healing must face emotional challenges without shielding, gradually learning to cope with them. Although it is a time-consuming process, avoiding these energies without remorse is a more effective and enduring strategy, known as the non-attachment technique in the empath healing journey.

Conclusion

Empathy, often interchangeably referred to as sympathy, is delineated as a mental phenomenon encompassing the capacity to genuinely envision the emotional encounters of others. It involves the ability to comprehend the extent of suffering in someone feeling sad or disappointed, establishing a secure connection with an individual who has been betrayed or unfairly offended, or resonating with the triumph of a person who has successfully accomplished a task. An empathetic individual appears to share analogous experiences with others.

At first glance, the concept of experience may seem uncomplicated, as our shared or nearly identical experiences should, in theory, allow us to understand the emotions of others by recalling our own reactions in similar situations. However, behaviors guided by empathy are surprisingly infrequent. The scarcity of empathy is underscored by instances such as a psychologist investigating post-World War II trials against Nazi officials, where the root of the horrifying capacity to commit atrocities was identified as a lack of empathy. In such extreme cases, individuals view others as mere soulless numbers and figures.

While extreme, this lack of empathy is not limited to historical atrocities. In everyday life, numerous "small" cases involve the infliction or receipt of harm through inappropriate words, contempt, arrogance, or disrespect. In both instances, the common denominator is selfishness, wherein individuals either consider themselves the sole importance deserving of sympathy or, at the very least, perceive themselves as the "center of the world" to which others must conform.

Interactions with family, friends, colleagues, and romantic partners heavily hinge on one's social skills. Empathy, therefore, becomes a crucial element in building effective social skills. It is inherent in human nature to feel and, in certain situations, to offer assistance. Although empathy is not foolproof and may falter, it plays a vital role in human social lives. People who experience empathy are more inclined to engage in pro-social behaviors, benefiting other individuals significantly.

Empathy is defined as "the ability to acknowledge and share the feelings and experiences of another person." Essentially, it involves putting oneself in someone else's shoes, comprehending and feeling what they go through, and envisioning the world from their perspective. Understanding someone's actions or behavior becomes possible only by imagining oneself in their position, walking in their shoes, and considering things from their point of view.

Empathy is not universally experienced; some individuals can detach from distressing news stories, such as terrorist attacks, and easily fall asleep. Contrastingly, a substantial percentage of people find it challenging to watch the same news, as it evokes deep feelings of pain and suffering, preventing them from falling asleep. Empathy is characterized as "the psychological identification with or vicarious experience of another person's emotions, feelings, or attitudes." It is crucial to differentiate between empathy and sympathy, where sympathy involves expressing comfort or sorrow for someone else's suffering without necessarily comprehending their struggles or life perspective.

www.ingramcontent.com/pod-product-compliance
Lightning Source LLC
LaVergne TN
LVHW011953070526
838202LV00054B/4911